~~WRITE~~ RIGHT FROM GOD

YOU, WORDS, WRITING AND YOUR DIVINE PURPOSE

TOM BIRD

Sojourn Publishing, LLC books are available
for order through Ingram Press Catalogues

Tom Bird
Visit my website at www.tombird.com

Printed in the United States of America
First Printing: December 2014
Published by Sojourn Publishing, LLC

ISBN: 978-1-62747-112-1

Introduction

"In the beginning was the Word, and the Word was with God, and the Word was God." - John 1:1.

For centuries, humans beings have had an obsession with the written word.

In fact, it was Aristotle who believed that, to live a truly complete life, every human being needed to write a book.

In fact, so obsessed currently are we still with writing that, according to a *New York Times* article published in 2002, 81 percent of Americans felt that they had a book stuck in them that they needed to get out. (Epstein, Joseph, "Think You Have a Book in You? Think Again," *The New York Times*, September 28, 2002. Accessed March 11, 2015. http://www.nytimes.com/2002/09/28/opinion/think-you-have-a-book-in-you-think-again.html.)

Could something or someone of a greater, all seeing, all knowing nature and purpose be trying to establish a direct connection with us through luring us into a communion through an association with the written word?

I think so.

At least that is what I have seen over and over and over again, in my thirty-two years of work with those who have been led, drawn, pushed, carried, and dragged to write books. Most of these individuals had previously suppressed this innate urge by trying to read their lives away. After finally giving in though, and utilizing the divinely-led method available to all of us, they wrote the books that were "stuck inside of them." All areas of their lives grew and changed for the better, and seemingly overnight. They healed relationships and wounds of all sorts. They uncovered a directness of purpose, leading to

"I know God will not give me anything I can't handle. I just wish that He didn't trust me so much."
MOTHER TERESA

"Believe nothing, no matter where you read it, or who said it – even if I have said it – unless it agrees with your own reason and your own common sense."
BUDDHA

"I always say, keep a diary and someday it'll keep you."
MAE WEST

"Do not fear death so much, but rather the inadequate life."
BERTOLT BRECHT

"If at first the idea is not absurd, then there is no hope for it."
ALBERT EINSTEIN

an opportunity for greater influence and peace. And they realized a greater ability to love and be loved than any had ever thought imaginable.

If those around you are encouraging you to write a book, they have been doing so for a reason greater than you can imagine. If your mind is constantly wandering off in the direction of best seller lists, something is desperately trying to get your attention. If you are a voluntary, avid reader of books, something greater than your humanity is reaching out to you. If an inspiration to write overtakes you, for whatever reason, at a variety of times and places, that inspiration is attempting to lock into you for the greatest of all human purposes.

If any of the above sounds like you, read on and ready yourself to take the transformational journey and understanding of a lifetime......Tom Bird

Chapter One
My Story

You may wonder both how it is that I came to write this book and what qualifies me to write it in the first place. Both are fair and justifiable questions. Both deserve direct answers, as well. For if you are going to place your faith in me, in what will become obvious, as you read on, as a very pivotal aspect of your life, it is essential that you understand who I am, where I come from, and from where I have derived the information that I share in this book.

Let me address the last portion of the aforementioned statement first. Over the last thirty-two years, in one way or another, I have worked with over 80,000 would-be authors. They came in all shapes and forms, young, more seasoned, rich, not so rich, highly educated, not so formally educated. So, they were a very diverse bunch. However, one thing that they had in common was that they either felt as if they were being pushed to write a book or actually, consciously wanted to do so. Most didn't feel prepared or qualified to do so. In one way or another, some consciously and some unconsciously, all suffered from the "Who would want to read what I write anyway?" syndrome. I worked with them in a variety of ways, whichever way suited them best, through one-night lectures, longer classes, weeklong retreats, weekend retreats. Whatever.

Aside from my professional credentials, what really qualified me to work with them and guide them through the process of writing and publishing their books was that I had once been like them.

"Style is the man himself."
COMTE de BUFFON

"To express that which God has conceived for him should be man's great purpose in life."
BAIRD T. SPALDING;
Life and Teaching of the Masters of the Far East

I was born in Erie, Pennsylvania, in 1956, a highly dysfunctional time in our greatly dysfunctional country. I was the fifth of five children, with two full sisters and two stepsisters from my father's previous failed marriage to an alcoholic wife; thus, I was the only boy and the youngest by nine years.

Despite the life-changing wisdom my father would come to share with me, both of my parents were just tired. Tired of parenting, tired of each other, dog-tired of the life they had chosen to lead.

By the time I was born, my mother had become a ball of anger and that anger ruled the roost. Even though she had always been seen as an angry woman, by the time I was born, it was blazing out of control. She would later convey to me, after she had passed over, that anger was all she had to offer life. And after I was born, anger was all she had to offer as a parent. This anger would eventually lead her to try to poison me to death when I was fourteen years old.

In an attempt at marginally responsible parenting, my mother kept her distance from me as a baby. From her perspective, branding me with a substantial abandonment wound was the lesser of two evils, especially when one considers what she was truly capable of, as evidenced by what she would consciously try to do to me at fourteen. Thus, I was not held as a child. And my mother immediately turned her volatile, ruthless anger toward anyone who tried to give me the affection babies normally receive and experience, including my father.

You could say that I grew up alone, but that would not be totally true. In fact, far from it. Other children experienced that immediate transference of bonding with God, Spirit, Source, Whoever you refer to He/She/It (for the purpose of this book and for simplicity's sake, I will just refer to this Almighty as God), to bonding with their parents. I never experienced that transference. My mother's resentfulness and anger kept that from happening. It was, of course, a very painful thing to be born into the world with no parent there to greet me—to love me. That wound haunts me to this day. However, on the other hand, it was a blessing. For while other children transferred their dependence of love and support from God to their parents, I never let go of that innate, direct connection with God, which is available to all of us. And it would be this infallibility that would lead me to survive my upbringing, including my mother's attempt to murder me, and guide me to any and all personal successes that I would achieve in my life.

It was in those long periods of time, in being left alone, deserted by my parents, that I would relax into the soft, caring, and reassuring comfort of my direct connection with God. As I got older and could spend more and more time away from my parents' house, I began to openly seek those quiet and uninterrupted moments I had come to rely on as a young child. Every day I would steal away, sometimes just for a few minutes, more often for hours, to make time to sink into the softness and safety of what I consider to be the ultimate of all connections for us all, which ties directly into the premise of what this book is all about.

With that direct connection leading the way, I knew what I wanted to do when I was very young. The direction of my life was unclouded by any aspirations my parents could have had for me. The road was open for the Source, by which I was being raised directly to bring to my attention the true direction my soul was guiding me to take. As a result, by the age of six, when I was just starting

"Creative activity could be described as a type of learning process where the teacher and the pupil are located in the same individual."
ARTHUR KOESTLER

"Great men are they who see that spiritual is stronger than any material force and that thoughts rule the world."
EMERSON

"There is surely a piece of divinity in us, something that was before the elements."
THOMAS BROWNE

3

*"You can't build a
reputation on what
you're going to do."*
HENRY FORD

to read, I knew, unequivocally, what I wanted to do with my life. I wanted to write.

Now, I grew up in a hardworking, labor-till-you-drop, blue-collar family and city. So, the idea of being a writer, specifically an author, was seen as a pipe dream. Writing was something one planned to do after the bills had been paid, the kids graduated from school, and the house was paid off. It was what you did after the life had been literally squeezed out of you by overworking at whatever job you hated to do. Writing was not something that you did for a vocation.

However, the older I got, the more independent I became and the more I consciously relied on what I perceived as a direct connection with God. As a result, I cared less and less about what my parents, friends, and town would think. In response, the spirit of God grew stronger in me each day. And I received the final clarification I needed just a few months after my mother's attempt to take my life.

*"The Son consciousness
causes the fulfillment;
the servant
consciousness causes
the lack."*
BAIRD T. SPALDING;
*Life and Teaching of the
Masters of the Far East*

It was late on a warm summer evening, around 2 a.m., when I exited my parents' house, as I so often did to slip into the solace of the night, where the ultimate quiet could be found, where I would also find the clearest of all channels available to me to best hear God. All of us have the ability to commune directly with God. We can all feel God, who is always reaching out to us, in feelings, visions, dreams, lyrics to songs, whatever. I feel God communicating to me in a variety of ways. And due to my dysfunctional upbringing, I may feel it more than most.

On the whole, I am more kinesthetic by nature. My ability to feel things outdoes the effect of even the visions I see in my mind. So, the most natural and effective form of communication between God and me is through the feelings I feel.

So it was, on this one summer evening, with the reassuring sound of the leaves on the tall willows that surrounded our yard gently blowing in the wind, I laid down, relaxing into the soft grass of my parents' side yard, and gazed into the clear night sky. I was so used to communing with God on late nights such as that one. I couldn't have felt any more comfortable that evening with myself, with everything around me, or especially in my connection with God. I couldn't have felt any more at ease or at home.

That evening, as so often before, I came to that communing with something on my heart. In most cases, I wouldn't recognize what it was that the Almighty and I would be communing for the evening; I simply could feel its emotional weight. On that specific evening, I could tell that I would be dealing with an issue of extraordinarily great significance.

As I laid there, softly and calmly, I could feel the issue for that evening gradually enter into my consciousness. In response, I felt my body embrace it and immediately I saw an image appear in my mind. My family, their lifestyles, and our family home. Off to the side, away from them, I stood, as if I was separate from them.

It was this vision, and the feelings it stirred in me, that catalyzed the topic for that evening to arise in my consciousness. And though it entered gently, it was still a big issue. It came in at full force, which helped me to realize the magnitude of what was entering me.

At that exact moment, the topic of discussion for that evening between God and me became crystal clear. At that moment, as well, I could see that I had been struggling with this age-old issue my entire life. It was at that time, too, that the words came.

"I will work in my own way, according to the light that is in me."
LYDIA MARIA CHILD

"There is the risk you cannot afford to take [and] there is the risk you cannot afford to take."
PETER DRUCKER

"I am so different from my family, God, that it scares me, causing me to wonder if somehow a mistake had been made and that I was delivered into the wrong family. I mean, they are good people and I love them, but we are just so different. They are focused on paying bills and I tend to be focused on what I feel is a different, bigger purpose, and the simple act of making money just doesn't seem to be enough, fulfilling to me."

"Which brings me to the following concerns, Lord. My goals in life appear so different from those of my family, that I tend to question the validity of what it is that I want to do with my life. I question why it is that I want to write. I feel unworthy to do so and if the influence of the family I was born into is an indicator of the direction I am meant to follow with my life, then I shouldn't be even considering writing as a profession."

In that moment, I could feel that God had been waiting, for what seemed like an eternity, for me to bring this subject to the table. Thus, the initial response I felt to my question came in the form of a heavenly sigh, as if God was saying something to the effect of, "Thank God (ha ha), that he has finally brought this topic to bear with me."

It was as if God's words were moving through me like a melody vibrating through a tuning fork, strong, yet soft, and crystal clear. I felt God's response.

"Tom—" The message stopped a moment for emphasis. "The reason you are drawn to write is because you see life as such a beautiful thing. And when you write, the people who read your writing will be able see life through your eyes and how you see it."

The effect of those simple, direct words, of that communion that night, still ring true with me today. As I write this, I recall how I felt that night, almost as if I were back there, right here and right now.

A few days later, as if he had been picking up on the message I was given, and building upon God's response, my father sat down with me and initiated the only serious, completely heartfelt conversation of our time together. A soft, sensitive, compassionate man, my father was taking a big step. By doing so, he would be certainly risking the penetrating wrath of my always angry, borderline mother. So looking back, I appreciate now even more the amount of love and caring my father must have had for me that day to do what he did. As well, in a very deep way, I could see from the conversation that we had that day, as if God was speaking through my father, how much he truly loved and cared for me.

Our conversation dealt with a job I had taken as a cashier at an always-busy discount supermarket nearby. My father sacrificed himself to support his family. And when it would all be said and done, he ended up working for forty-eight years at a job he despised. But in the very moment of our conversation, I could see that my father had found the key to life.

"Son," he said, "you're too young to start working. You should be just enjoying life, getting to know yourself. So that you can find out what it is that you want to do with your life, which is really the key to living a happy life. And that's what life is all about. Find out what it is that you want to do with your life. Now is the time to do that. Then, just do that. And you will be the best at whatever it is that you choose to do, because you will love it. So don't worry about money or a career. Don't let them be your focus. Focus instead on what you love to do and the money and career will follow."

A few months afterward, I was drawn to a magazine—I think it was *Psychology Today*—which featured a story on Maslow's Hierarchy of Needs.

"God is love, but get it in writing."
GYPSY ROSE LEE

"Far better it is to dare mighty things, to win glorious triumphs even though checkered by failure, than to rank with those poor spirits who neither enjoy nor suffer much because they live in the gray twilight that knows neither victory or defeat."
THEODORE
ROOSEVELT

7

"The test of any man lies in action."

PINDAR,
522-433 B.C.

In short, Dr. Abraham Maslow believed that the key to having a successful life was living a happy one. To give his innovative theory greater foundation, Maslow took to the study of so-called "happy people." He hoped to find some commonalities between happy people, that the rest of us could follow, to best emulate their collective successes at the game referred to as life.

What Maslow discovered was that each one of the individuals he studied had a period of social disobedience, where each one stood up to the mores of society, to give himself the time necessary to see who he was and what he really wanted to do with his life, so he could do it.

Riding on the wings of the clarity I received, both from God and my father's advice, I immediately put into play my own plan of social disobedience as prescribed by Maslow. This translated to taking off from life, school, whatever to go in search of who I really was and what it was that I really wanted to do with my life. I went to school just so I could graduate, but I refused to do any assignments whatsoever. Long story short, I went from being an honor student to being a just-scraping-by-guy. However, looking back, I wouldn't trade the decision I made for anything. For, because of my actions over those three years of high school, on a necessary human level, I solidified the recognition of my life purpose, and was fully and finally able to commit to it with all of my earthly heart and soul.

"Style is knowing who you are, what you want and want to say, and not giving a damn."

GORE VIDAL

Thank God for open admission universities, though. There is no way that I would have gotten into a school without them. I eventually chose Slippery Rock State University, in Slippery Rock, Pennsylvania, nestled in the desolate, rolling hills of Western Pennsylvania, about forty-five miles north of Pittsburgh. "The Rock" was a former teachers' college and had transformed into one of the top Physical Education universities in the country by the time I stepped onto campus in 1975. But it also had a good English Department and was my top choice amongst all of the other state schools that were available to me.

Before I even officially stepped on campus, though, I had to go through New Student Orientation, which was a collection of activities to get us fully ready for and used to being a full-time college student. We were also asked to take some placement tests, to see how well-prepared we were for some of the mandatory entry level classes, and to see which ones we were proficient enough to pass out of. Even though I had not cracked a book in three years, I still graded out in the top 2 percent of entry level university students in communication skills, which, of course, was just further confirmation that I was on the right track with regard to the direction I had chosen to follow with my life.

I really thrived during my time at The Rock. I had already gotten the sowing of my wild oats out of the way. And during that, I had given myself the space and time to fully embrace what my life was calling me to do. Eventually, in 1979, the English Department elected me as their Senior of the Year, when I graduated with honors in both English and Psychology.

After graduation from The Rock in 1979, it was off to an internship with the Pittsburgh Pirates. I actually started the job about two months before graduation, on Opening Day in April of that year. The Pirates, the famous Family led by charismatic future Hall of Famer, and one of my best friends, Willie Stargell, won the World Series in my first year with the team, and I was offered a full-time position as their Assistant Director of Publicity. As fine of a job as my position with the team was, I grew progressively unhappy as the years passed, because I was not living my heartfelt dream as an author.

"In no other period of history were the learned so mistrusted of the divine possibilities in man as they are now."
GOPI KRISHNA

"Words are not just containers but containers of energy."
PAUL FERRINI;
Reflections of the Christ Mind

My time with the club was valuable, though. The time I was able to invest pursuing my dream of becoming an author was not a total waste, because I spent whatever free moments I had doing exactly that. I tried and tested everything I had been taught at The Rock with regard to becoming the author I already felt I was. I read every book I could get my hands on, covering the topics of writing, editing, getting published, whatever. I even had the opportunity to be in the company of many a famous sportswriter and author, all of whom had already succeeded at the art which I was dying to be a part of. However, by my fourth year with the club, I had become exceedingly depressed because none of what I had read, been taught, or told about succeeding as an author was bearing any fruit in my life.

Finally, after a weekday night game in Pittsburgh, I had had it. I couldn't take it any more. Not only had I grown to despise my job but I was angry at myself for not doing a better job of pursuing what I had come to the planet to do vocationally. When I got home to my one-bedroom apartment that night, I collapsed in a bundle of tears. I had reached my wit's end. As hard as I had tried and much as I had learned, nothing I had acquired, not personal advice, nothing, had gotten me any closer to achieving my dream. Finally, I dropped to my knees and had the mother of all conversations with God, with whom I had neglectfully stopped communing as soon as I joined the Pirates.

Desperation is certainly the forefather of faith. Well, at least it was for me that special evening. For it was the desperation that I was feeling at that moment that eventually dropped me to my knees. There, I continued to weep and started to pray. In my prayers that evening I expressed my heartfelt concerns and pain.

"I know, God, that I want to become an author," I said. "And I know you want the same for me, as well. But nobody down here seems to know how to go about becoming one. There's no absolute route, no two plus two equals four."

I paused for a moment before continuing.

I continued hesitantly because I did not feel worthy to receive what it was that I was going to be asking for, "I promise God, that if you show me how to succeed as an author that I will always devote time, for the rest of my life, to sharing whatever it is that you share with me."

Shortly after saying that I collapsed in a heap on my living room floor and fell fast asleep.

Two nights later, in the middle of the night, I awoke in a semi-dream state. While in that dream state, an abbreviated version, dealing with authoring, flashed before my eyes. I was being shown how I had been prepared to live my life as an author, everything from the connection with God that I had never lost, to the psychology and philosophy classes I had taken while at The Rock. I could see that these classes were far more pertinent to my success as an author than all of the writing classes I had taken. I could see all the way to the desperate state that had caused me to make my tearful plea a few nights before. It was all there, including the step-by-step plan I had requested, that I needed to put into play, and I began to do so the following morning. That plan focused on re-communing with God through my writing. Once I did that, and in the manner which I had been shown, the results I had been longing for began to materialize rapidly in my life.

A few days after I had made my heartfelt plea, I could see, as clearly as my hand in front of my own face, exactly where it was that I needed to go initially with my writing.

"Everyone is in the best seat."

JOHN CAGE

"Your path has its own simple beauty and mystery."

PAUL FERRINI;
*Reflections of the
Christ Mind*

11

"I can say 'I am terribly frightened and fear is terrible and awful and it makes me uncomfortable, so I won't do that because it's uncomfortable. It is uncomfortable doing something that's risky.' But so what? Do you want to stagnate and just be comfortable?"
BARBRA STREISAND

Not only could I see where I was meant to go, but I could also see that I was being led, pushed, and dragged in that direction. I finally approached my old buddy, the most beloved professional athlete in the United States at the time—Willie Stargell—about writing his story. Even though, Willie had sworn off ever going down that road again due to a bad previous experience, he accepted my offer to co-author his autobiography. As he said, "You are the only person in the world that I trust to do that with." Willie gave me carte blanche to do whatever was necessary to make his book a reality.

Two days later, I landed legendary Literary Agent Scott Meredith as our representative for the book. More than anyone else, Scott ran the world of book publishing. A few weeks later, and a total of about six weeks, all told, from when I had made my initial plea and put into play the plan I had seen in my dream, Scott sold the rights to my first book to Harper & Row. Harper & Row was the third largest publishing house in the world at that time. The advance was equivalent to three times my annual salary, and enabled me to finally resign from my position with the team and take to writing full-time. At the ripe old age of twenty-six, I had landed the mother of all dreams for myself of becoming a full-time author. All of this came, I feel, as the result of reconnecting directly back to God through my writing; and this became a huge life-changer for me.

Chapter Two
Lessons Learned

I kept true to my word and began teaching shortly afterward. After a bit of experimentation in regard to how I would do so, I decided that I would design and then begin teaching courses, specifically geared toward persons who embodied the type of confusion and desperation, demonstrated by the wayward, would-be author I had been. Much to my surprise, there were far more would-be authors hungry for the information I had to share than I ever could have imagined, enough to carry me through over 4600 classes taught and lectures given, at over 120 colleges and universities, over the next twenty-three years that followed.

Because the culture had been programmed through centuries of fickle conditioning to believe that writing a good book was impossible for most and darn right hard, difficult and grueling for the blessed few, I had to start out slowly, by offering courses on how to write one's book in a year. Believe it or not, it was a massive stretch for people to believe even that was possible. Oh, how far we've come. Over time, as our culture generally seemed to open its heart more fully to its own potential, I was able to shorten the time-frames of my classes to match titles such as Write Your Book in 90 Days, and then Forty-five Days and then Thirty Days.

The road eventually led me to convert my teaching from primarily being class and lecture based to a retreat format. I would be leading, one-on-one, a collection of aspiring authors through the writing of what was, in most cases, their first books. And by doing so, I would be able to stay

"Grasshopper, look beyond the game, as you look beneath the surface of the pool to see its depths."
MASTER PO, KUNG FU

"The spiritual path culminates when you fully realize your God, nature, and that of all the other beings around you."
PAUL FERRINI; *Reflections of the Christ Mind*

home a whole lot more. Little did I know how amazing of an experience this would be for all involved, especially me, and how big of a leap this would entail with regard to a soul understanding of what I had been teaching for over the last two decades. Most of that soul understanding would come as the result of actually witnessing the results, right before my very eyes. Little did I know, as well, how much I would learn about the true essence of the craft and the actual process, on which I had been sharing information for decades, and that that knowledge would result from the natural approach to delivery that we took with the birth of our loving daughter, Skyla.

As it seems I always do, I started out conservatively by offering a few Write Your Book in Eight Days Retreats, which worked amazingly well. The only problem was that those in attendance finished the writing of their books in an average of three days, which I thought provided a great opportunity to get their second books completed at the retreat, as well. Unfortunately, those in attendance at my retreats didn't share my perspective. They were so excited that they had finally completed the writing of their long-awaited books, that all they wanted to do was celebrate.

In my next conservative move, I decided to shorten the book-writing retreat to five days, but we ran into the same problem. Authors were still completing the writing of their books in an average of just under three days. So, finally, I bit the bullet and converted my retreats to "Write Your Book in a Weekend" offerings.

It was from the results of those weekend retreats that I could actually witness the true magnitude of what I had been led to share. At those retreats, I could see the power of the inspiration pouring through the lives, souls, and bodies of those in attendance, bringing them amazing personal and professional results.

Here's what I witnessed and discovered at my retreats, time and time and time again.

First of all, I don't teach anyone how to write a book, much like you can't teach anyone how to go through the act of birthing a child naturally. All you can do is instruct them on the phases that will transpire, so they can best go with the flow. Then, you just need to create a stable, safe environment, void of all distractions, for them to go through the natural birthing or release process all on their own, which is exactly what I do. But never, never, never, despite several hundred, if not thousands, of requests to do so, do I ever bias their divine, individual experiences by telling anyone how to write their books. What I do instead is focus on setting the stage for them, clearing any resistance in advance, by walking them through the stages shared by all who are engaged in their book-birthing. Once familiar with these steps, it becomes much easier for them to go with the natural flow of the process, as opposed to viewing it all from a negative perspective and rejecting it in its entirety.

None of the above would have worked in any way, shape, or form, if my authors had to create a book. For just like a mother giving birth, they too were releasing something that had already been created. For as I witnessed time and time again, there was no creation associated with the writing of the authors' books at my retreats. Instead, they were simply releasing that which had obviously been created beforehand. Each one of their books, like a child, seemed to have a life of its own. As books came flying out of my authors, they would often come out in forms greatly different than anything my writers ever could have imagined. Then, after each of my authors in attendance gave up trying to control the experience and instead just gave into it, each was taken on

"A man does not have to be an angel in order to be a saint."
ALBERT SCHWEITZER

"God tells me how He wants this music played – and you get in His way."
ARTURO TOSCANINI

> *"I'm only the Pope, what can I do?"*
> POPE JOHN XXIII

a life-altering ride, as the book dipped and climbed and meandered rapidly around twists, turns, and curves, much like a world-class roller coaster, before coming to a rapid halt, seemingly out of nowhere.

None of this would have been possible, of course, if the book had not already have been a full and complete entity unto itself, way before it was released through the lives of my authors. This gives credence to why so many of my attendees felt pushed, pulled, and dragged to write a book for so long, both internally and by friends, family, and colleagues. For if the books that a prospective author has within already exist with the soul purpose of being birthed into life, would it not make sense that, like a baby in the third trimester, it would seek to be born? This is exactly what I have witnessed at my retreats. Authors come in, usually with a desperate desire to get their books out of them, much like an expectant mother a few days from her due date. And after giving into the process, the baby actually births itself, as assisted by the mother, who sets the stage. This experience, which I see consistently at my retreats, mirrors the results of that statistic quoted in *The New York Times*, which stated that 81 percent of all Americans believe that "they have a book in them" that they have to get out.

So stay with me on this next point, because it is the most important pearl of wisdom that I convey in this book.

> *"What God does, He does well."*
> JEAN de LaFONTAINE

Let's take as true, that an aspiring author has a book inside of him, and that when opened up, books come barreling through that author in the form of rapid writing inspiration. Then, wouldn't it make sense that a book may actually be a spiritual entity in its own right, much like a newborn baby?

Let's further take as true, that that book may have actually been authored by the actual author, and that this was carried out in conjunction with God, while the actual would-be author was in what I like to refer to as the other side of life. Then, wouldn't it also make sense that the book was actually written there, in that place on the other side of life, before the would-be author, who will release the book into life, was actually born?

And then, if this book-to-be-released has actually been written by the would-be author in conjunction with, or at least in the presence of, God, while on the other side of life, when the author births or releases that book into life, in its spiritual entirety, wouldn't it carry with it the direct, communal, divine, and spiritual elements common on the other side of life? Couldn't that book bear qualities representative of God's own attributes?

If we can take these as truths, wouldn't they all attest to the reason behind the massive personal healing and advances experienced by authors who employ the system that I have been led to share at my retreats? Can we now comprehend more fully how lives, relationships, and often physical ailments are routinely healed and seem to correlate directly with the authoring of books at my retreats?

And further, would it not then make sense, that the divinely-led, spiritual entity we frequently refer to as a book, like a baby conceived and readied to be born, would also have a special time when it was geared and prepared to arrive on this planet? Can we perceive its perfect timing, that not only best facilitates the release of its message into *this* side of life, but also the timely healing of its author, the vehicle, who also agreed to have that book come through?

This is pretty deep stuff. So you may want to re-read the last six paragraphs one or more times, before moving on to the next chapter.

"We need some imaginative stimulus, some not impossible ideal such as may shape vague hope, and transform it into effective desire, to carry us year after year, without disgust, through the routine work which is so large a part of life."
WALTER PATER,
1885

"If God did not exist, it would not be necessary to invent Him."
VOLTAIRE

Chapter Three
And the Word was....

Beginning with the great works of Gabrielle Rico (Tarcher), Julia Cameron (Tarcher), and Natalie Goldberg (Bantam) for decades, the healing aspects of writing have become well-known. Journaling has become a mainstay in work with patients in therapy and other emotional healing modalities. But no one has yet been able to explain why the actual writing process has become such an effective way to heal.

This chapter will do exactly that, as well as explain the keys to the unacknowledged transformational aspects of writing.

"It is the chiefest point of happiness that a man is willing to be what he is."
DESIDERIUS ERASMUS; 1465-1536

"In the beginning was the Word, and the Word was with God, and the Word was God." - John 1:1.

The above line pretty much says it all. When you connect with the Word through your writing, especially the authoring of your book, you are given the greatest opportunity to rapidly get back on your divine life path. You are allowing God to stream directly into your life, and the positive changes that result to you and your life can be massive. At least this is what I have seen on a consistent basis, time and time again, in my intense thirty years of work with aspiring authors.

"God is subtle but He is malicious."
ALBERT EINSTEIN

Does that mean that the only way to connect with God through writing is by writing your book? No. As many of you have experienced through your other forms of writing, especially journaling, that is not the case. However, when one connects with God through the more extensive time

"If we weren't all crazy, we would all go insane."
JIMMY BUFFETT

"Tis God gives skill, but not without men's hands. He could not make Antonio Stradivarius' violin without Antonio."
STRADIVARIUS

commitment of writing a book, more surfaces for the author than the substantial healing aspects of writing itself. The more intensive time commitment, combined with the method I feel destined to share, enables the author of the book to move beyond simple healing into real-life transformation on both the personal and professional levels. This is something uniquely special to the act of writing a book using the divine method that was initially shared with me. But I do not feel it is unavailable to other art forms, which utilize similarly intensive, long-term time commitments. This makes the combination of connecting with God through the writing of a book, and in conjunction with the divine method I share, so transformational and, thus, so super-special.

For by doing so, not only are you guaranteed to remain in a direct communion with God for an extended period of time, but, most of all, through the writing of a book, you birth into life first your divine voice and then the message you were meant to deliver. And whether that message affects the life of only one reader, who then affects millions, or your book directly affects millions, nothing could be more soulfully fulfilling.

As well, keep in mind that no matter what type of writing you have done up to this point, none of it has been wasted. All writing, like a stream flowing into a river, which flows to the ocean, is designed to bring you back to God and, thus back to yourself through the writing of your book. Nothing is more exciting, thrilling, and fulfilling than the release of one's soul purpose and voice through the writing of one's book by means of the divine method I have devoted my life to sharing. And, if you are drawn to or being pushed in this direction, as I have witnessed firsthand thousands of times, you will not enjoy the peace you deserve until you have stepped beyond the boundaries of your false fears of unworthiness, or whatever, and completed the writing of your book through the divine method I teach.

What connecting to the Word entails is quite simple. What it translates to is simply getting out of our own way. When we quiet our frequently obsessive minds, amazing things transpire, including the writing of an entire book length manuscript in a weekend or less.

For God, Spirit, is always speaking to us, counseling us, and guiding us. And when we stop to listen, we fully integrate Him/Her/It into our lives and, again, innately amazing things, often referred to as miracles, transpire.

This, of course, is exactly what takes place when you write a book by the method I have been employing, both for my own personal use and in my work with aspiring authors, for over three decades. For being in unadulterated, complete, total, absolute communion with the Source for upwards of ten hours a day, over the course of a few days, life-changing events couldn't help but unfold. And they do. Not only do books get written, not only are bestselling authors released, but individuals, at the deepest of all soul levels, obtain healing. And when one heals, enlightenment finds room to come streaming through. All of these reasons make clear why so many individuals feel drawn to write a book.

Sure, the completion of a book is a huge blessing unto itself, but the process one goes through to write that book, if the proper method is employed to do so, could be even more rewarding. The great Aristotle understood the personal significance of the individual writing a book. This perspective also gives credence again to why, according to *The New York Times*, it was as true in his day as it is today for that 81 percent of Americans, who feel their books "stuck inside of them," books that they just have to get out.

"I did not write. God wrote it. I merely did His dictation."
HARRIET BEECHER STOWE

"You can have anything you want if you want it desperately enough. You must want it with an inner exuberance that erupts through the skin and joins the energy that created the world."
SHEILA GRAHAM

Chapter Four
A Challenge

Okay, let's say that there is something much more to be derived from the writing of a book than just the placing of words on paper or in a text file. And let's just say, as well, that everything does indeed happen for a reason and that there are no accidents, including your reading of this book. Let's take the further position that, just maybe, you were led to or pushed or brought forth to read this book because it was God's way of getting you to write your own book.

If the above were true, of course, it would be normal for several thoughts to arise on your end, such as, "But I don't feel like I have a book inside of me, so I don't really find myself wanting to write one." Or perhaps, "If writing a book is supposedly so God-led, such that we have an innate ability to do so, then why has it been so difficult for me to do so up to this point?"

In regard to the initial concern, "But I don't feel a book inside of me, so I don't really find myself wanting to write one."—I counter in response by asking the question, "Then why are you reading this book to begin with and why have you read this far if there isn't something going on with you in regard to this topic?" I mean, if that were truly the case with you, I am sure there are many more books that you could have read that would be far more interesting than this particular one.

Denial is a terrible thing to share with yourself, especially denial of your truest, most God-centered self, but let's face it—we all do it.

"Art is a collaboration between God and the artist, and the less the artist does the better."
ANDRE GIDE

"An adventure is only an inconvenience rightly considered."
G. K. CHESTERTON

I would guesstimate that 35 percent of those who attend my retreats enter under the banner of, "I have no idea why I am taking this retreat. I don't feel like there's a book inside of me and I really have no desire to write one."

Yet, they were still drawn to attend a retreat, just as you have been drawn to read this book. And, according to my recollections, each person who entered under the aforementioned banner, not only ended up writing a book at a retreat, but also got knocked out of their self imposed states of denial, to venture through their own deep, personal and spiritual transformations, to which God was obviously leading them through the penning of their manuscripts.

A word to the wise is sufficient.

Keep reading.

Now onto the second of the two obvious concerns represented by the challenge: "If the writing of a book is supposedly so God-led and thus we have an innate ability to do so, then why has it been so difficult for me to do so up to this point?"

Let's look at that. There are actually two appropriate responses.

First of all, as mentioned earlier in this book, and in direct response to that query, success did not materialize simply because the proper techniques for achieving success were not applied. It's as simple as that. You can't successfully change a tire if you show up with the wrong wrench. A summary of the God-led techniques I have promised to share are covered in the last few chapters of this book.

Secondly, the reason why so many writers have had such great difficulty in writing their books is because it just wasn't the right time when they attempted to do so.

That's right. just like trying to birth a baby before it is ready to born, it simply wasn't the right time until right now, which is also why I feel that you are reading this book right now. There are no accidents or mistakes, you know.

In my How to Write Your Best Seller in a Weekend lectures, and retreats of the same name, I always start out by asking attendees to create an image in their minds that regresses them back to the time and place when they first realized that writing was something that they wanted to do. Most go back several years; some retreat back decades. And in doing so, they almost all experience the regret that has stood in their way of really writing for years.

They didn't understand what they received at that time—a feeling, a premonition that they would be writing. However, a premonition is a conscious prediction of an event to happen in the future. And just because they received a premonition, often through the caring eyes of another, they may have misinterpreted it as a calling for the present time. But it was not. It was a premonition, a roadmap, a street sign, pointing them in a direction of where they would be going, but were not meant to go at that time.

In fact, most everyone who attends one of my retreats or employs my method, after understanding the possibility about the premonition, is immediately able to release decades of guilt and frustration over the fact that they haven't yet published or even been writing.

And simply put, these individuals would not have been able to unload what often amounts to decades of guilt, in a mere instant of understanding, if this had not been the case.

"My dear, I don't care what they do, so long as they don't do it in the street and frighten the horses."
MRS. PATRICK CAMPBELL

"The kingdom of heaven may be compared to a man who sowed good seed in his field."
MATTHEW 13:24

So, what I am saying is that, back then, you probably couldn't have written and completed your book successfully, even if you'd wanted to.

There is this wonderful thing called karma that has gotten a really bad name, especially in the arena of divine timing. A layperson's definition of divine timing is nothing more and nothing less than when something of a divine nature, such as the writing of a book, is being divinely led to happen, when all of the stars line up, when wise men and women show up for a birth—that type of thing.

Karma is the older sibling of divine timing. By that, I mean that the former protects the latter.

How does it do that?

Karma protects divine timing by preventing the action that is meant to be taken from being completed until the exact time when it is meant to happen for maximum effectiveness.

In essence, karma keeps an aspiring author busy with his "stuff," until just the exact moment to birth a book.

And then, the aspiring author either stumbles upon or is led, in what usually seems like the most unusual of routes (Spirit just works that way), to the precise answers to solve those age-old dilemmas that have kept them from writing their books.

So, in building upon the first answer I shared to the questions that led off this chapter, most of these dilemmas simply deal with how people were taught to approach writing, which was from a purely intellectual point of view. As a result, they end up taking the opposite approach to actually and successfully writing their books. These books have been trying to burn a hole through their authors' brains, because writing is actually—and in this order of importance—a spiritual, emotional, intellectual, and physical art form.

By following what they were taught, and attempting to write a book from a purely intellectual perspective, they limit themselves to engage in only one of the four essential facets of writing, and the second-lowest ranking influence, at that. Doing so is like trying to drive a car on three flat tires.

Now, back to my response to the second question posed in this section (because responses to both questions actually do intersect). My extensive experience in working with aspiring authors has shown me that any lack of success they have experienced prior to our work together, has come as the result of it not being the right time, which directly coincides with the delivery of the right methodology as well.

And, as mentioned, now is the right time because you were drawn to read this book. And the frustration that has built up in you, as the result of any failures you may have potentially experienced with your writing, has gotten you to this point.

Yes, you heard me correctly.

No one ever really makes any substantial changes in life until pain or frustration forces them to.

So, yes, I am saying that any failure you may have experienced in the area of writing has led you to the doorway of your eventual success.

That's right. If that weren't the case, you wouldn't be here. But, now that you are, I can show you the way to harness all of the facets brought together by writing, to drive that car, fast and true, down the Autobahn of an experience, and across the finish line to the completion of your book.

"We can secure other people's approval, if we do right and try hard; but our own is worth a hundred of it."
MARK TWAIN

"Teach your children that they will never be judged, that they need not worry about always getting it right, and that they do not have to change anything, or 'get better,' to be seen as perfect and beautiful in the eyes of God."
NEALE DONALD WALSCH;
Communion with God

*"My parents have been
visiting me for a few
days. I just dropped
them off at the airport.
They leave tomorrow."*
MARGARET SMITH

But I can't do so until we take the first step to remove the conscious, emotional blocks that have been placed in your way, and now need to be removed, because it is your time to fully experience the full gamut of blessings available to you through the writing of your book(s) through the divinely led method I have been led to share.

Turn to the next chapter.

Chapter Five

Understanding and Then Removing the Origins of Our Resistance to Communing Directly With God

If you can, just for a moment, close your eyes and then take a few clearing, relaxing breaths. Do this until you feel completely relaxed and open. Once there, allow a big, soft, acknowledging smile to grace your face.

Your soul is directing you to a place with which you are intimately familiar. It is a place that, even though you may not consciously recognize it, it is still so familiar that it feels like home.

As you ease back into this most special of places, like slipping into the soft cushions of a favorite easy chair, you notice that you are surrounded by by tens of millions of soft, living books, all neatly and comfortably aligned on bookshelves. These books represent every topic imaginable and are of various shapes, sizes, and colors.

And all in a moment of notice, a shelf steps forward from among millions of other shelves, taking its place right before you. What makes this shelf so unique and special to you, is that it houses every book you have written, and potentially even co-authored with God. They were composed in this most pristine of spiritual environments, on this other side of life.

As you can now feel, your mission was not just to write these books, but to deliver them into life, while on the human side of existence.

As you can feel, at this very moment, each one of these books boasts of a uniquely special representation of the cornucopia of the ultimate message of life. As well, each

"When we were little we had no difficulty sounding the way we felt; thus, most little children speak and write with real voice."
PETER ELBOW;
Writing With Power

"Many people believe they are attracted by God, or by Nature, when they are only repelled by man."
DEAN INGE

*"All healing happens
thus: As illusions are
surrendered, truth
appears."*
PAUL FERRINI;
*Reflections of the
Christ Mind*

carries its own separate and individual personality, demeanor, and life force. Each is dying to be born, and will literally do anything necessary to live and fulfill its life mission. It will nag and cajole you relentlessly, until it is born into human existence.

As you slowly, carefully pull one of the books off the shelves, you feel it—the pain, the rejection and the resistance so often associated with the falling away of the façade, of the surface veneer, that severely limited who you truly are. When the façade is gone, your true identity can manifest in human form.

At that moment, you realize that the only person who has kept this from transpiring in your life up to this point, has been you and only you.

You realize at this time, as well, that the epicenter of your resistance is the false belief that, should you step into and embrace your truest of all identities while in human form, you will be rejected. Rejected by throngs of others. Rejected by people, who are not only frightened to take the step you are about to take, but so frightened, that these otherwise relatively nice individuals will go to all lengths to kill the messenger, when that messenger is only trying to deliver the message about who they really are.

This deep-seated fear within them has manifested in the form of a society, especially its churches, that have literally slaughtered, in one way or another, tens of millions, who have attempted, to bring through the divine truth about who we all truly are, as you are about to do.

You realize that there is one block that keeps you from releasing that book and its divine message, which you hold in your hands, into the human side of life. That one block is you and your belief that you will be persecuted, in one way or another, for taking this step forward. You realize

*"Let me assert my firm
belief that the only thing
we have to fear is fear
itself."*

FRANKLIN D.
ROOSEVELT

30

that the greatest persecution of all, your greatest fear, is the loss of love from those you love and on whom you depend for the love in your life.

***

On a conscious human level, what is it that has been most holding you back and sabotaging your efforts to write the book or books you are meant to write?

I realize that this may be the furthest thing from being true in other areas of your life. But in this one specific area, it is your fear of success that has been holding you back.

"What?" you're probably thinking. "You must be kidding me????? Are you nuts? Who would ever fail because of success?"

You, and yes, I am nuts. What's the line from that Jimmy Buffet song? "If we weren't all crazy we would all go insane?" So, I would rather be crazy or nuts. That way, I can keep myself from going insane.

Am I kidding you with this whole fear of success thing?

No.

When I first started teaching decades ago, I was not only amazed at the number of people who attended my classes, wanting to author books, but I was even more amazed at the degree of success that had already been achieved by most of my attendees.

My classes were jam-packed with CEOs from some of the largest corporations in the country, many of whom had acquired Master's degrees and Ph.D.s. Other participants had recovered from major illnesses, started their own businesses, or raised families and become great parents. You name it. They were in my audience.

What startled me most was that so many of them had

"The illusion of Failure is necessary in order to experience the exhilaration of Success."
NEALE DONALD WALSCH;
Communion with God

"Obstacles are those frightful things you see when you take your eyes off your goal."
HENRY FORD

been so successful in other areas of life which I considered to be much more challenging. Yet they had failed at something as God-given, God-directed and, at its root, as natural as breathing—writing.

Sure, educationally they had been innocently led astray by those who did not understand the essence of writing at that root level. Yet those teachers attempted with great devotion to teach us what they thought was the truth. The people who attended my classes were individuals whom I was sure had bucked the odds several times before in their lives. They had swum upstream, against the current of life, and succeeded. They had overcome many boundaries in their lives to accomplish what they had. Why then had they not succeeded with their writing, which appeared to be much more important to them than so many other successful endeavors?

I thought there must be some sort of internal block that was keeping them from really going after their writing dreams and moving beyond the educational misleads which they had all experienced. But what was that block?

I knew that if I could uncover what had kept these successful individuals from succeeding at the game of writing with the same vigor at which they had succeeded at the game of life, I would really be able to help them do something about it.

I decided to put the knowledge that I had acquired from over thirty hours of college coursework in psychology into action, conducting a survey with my student base designed to uncover what was internally holding these would-be authors back.

What I discovered astounded me and proved different from what I had expected. I discovered that, in the vast majority of those surveyed, their biggest controlling (and usually unconscious) fear was not a fear of failure, but rather—you guessed it—a fear of success.

Here are some examples—some extreme, some not—of the types of responses I received on my surveys. Some of these may resonate with you.

"If I am successful as an author, people will know more about me than I am comfortable with them knowing."

"People like the little guy. It's the guy with all of the fame and money that makes the front pages of tabloids, and if I am successful as a writer, that guy will be me."

"I've been living the same style of life for as long as I can remember. My life may not be everything I want it to be, but no one can guarantee me that it wouldn't be a heck of a lot worse if I were to go for it and succeed as an author."

"I may be seen as brilliant by some but crazy by others, if I were to really let people know who I was through the writing of a book."

"If I were to succeed as an author, I would be scared that those closest to me wouldn't be able to understand me anymore, or maybe I wouldn't be able to relate to them anymore. I would lose them and there is nothing I want more in my life than them."

"If I were to succeed as an author, I would be hounded by all types of responsibilities I don't have now. My life would no longer be my own."

"I would have to leave those I love to do what I want to do."

"For the first time in my life I would have something I would be scared to lose."

These would-be authors were afflicted, even by varying the degrees of severity, but to all of them, success at being a writer equated to becoming a strong catalyst for

"When you have to make a choice and don't make it, that in itself is a choice."
WILLIAM JAMES

"I ask you to recognize the fact that you have fear rising and that fear shuts down your heart."
PAUL FERRINI;
Reflections of the Christ Mind

33

change in their lives. Writing would bring them out of life's shadows and into the forefront. This would then open them up to some sort of put-downs or persecution. And in the worst cases, to the most daunting loss of all, that of the love of those closest to them, upon whom they personally depend. The successful would-be author holds a mirror up to those they most admire. But the would-be author worries about insulting these individuals, causing them to feel unworthy, incapable, inferior, or, worst of all, a failure. In time, these individuals would grow envious, both of the author's success and of the guts it requires to take the first steps. The author has felt all of these judgments in the past and anticipates these reactions from others in the future.

As consciously ridiculous as these fears may seem, even though they are mostly subconscious, they are very real. I know these fears, not only in my work with my beloved authors, but also in my own life.

Why would this be the case?

First of all, those who have strayed off their soul path get lost. They forget that life is a lot more than just holding down a job one hates and drinking or digging themselves an early grave through denial. They forget how wonderful and God-connected they really are, or possibly they never consciously knew.

"Those who give up on their dreams will discourage yours." - Bumper Sticker found on the back of my car.

When you embrace your own divinity—your purpose, your message, your voice, your path—that's a subconscious slap (good and hard, right across the face) to those who have given up on their dreams. If these individuals are not strong or brave enough internally to even be in touch with their own feelings and reactions to you, when they aren't strong enough to face themselves, all of those feelings and reactions are projected onto you. You get to be the bad guy.

Suddenly—immediately—you experience the ridicule and the put-downs of others, for taking the very brave step of being you, a step which most are too frightened to take. If we would all just stride into our own God-given divinity, racism, jealousy, hatred, and envy would soon become things of the past. We would no longer want what someone else had because we would all have what we needed.

To have everyone embrace their own individual divinity is a dream, but a worthy one. Writing a book is one way to take the step of clearing out all of the baggage that keeps every one of us from making room in our lives for our individual divinity and then allowing that divinity to have a direct form of expression through each one of us.

Possibly this is the reason so many are drawn to write books. Maybe doing so could end up being wildly more significant to each one of us than just putting words on paper.

It bears repeating. *The New York Times* claims that 81 percent of Americans feel as if they have a book stuck inside of them that they need to write.

And remember Aristotle, who believed that one of the three things every human being needed to do to live a full and complete life was to write a book.

Could the major reason that so many are drawn to write books, some kicking and screaming, be for the chance to receive the enlightenment and accompanying peace that we all seek?

My vast experience in this area has shown that to be the case, time and time and again. This is biggest reason I keep teaching after all of these years. Over the course of a short weekend, I have grown enamored of watching the

"The only service a friend can really render is to keep up your courage by holding up to you a mirror in which you can see a noble image of yourself."
GEORGE BERNARD SHAW

"Until you look in the mirror and see your own beliefs reflected there, you will be using every brother or sister in your experience as a mirror to show you what you believe about yourself."
PAUL FERRINI;
Reflections of the Christ Mind

birthing of a soul through the writing of a book. It just brings me the greatest of joys.

The second reason we fear our own success as writers is because we know the results. We have already experienced the damaging pain caused by the envy projected upon us by those in our lives, especially those we love most.

We have felt the wicked lashes of that envy slice through our hearts before and we don't want to feel it again. And we know that the attacks we receive in the future may cut and penetrate even more deeply than we've ever felt before—all because of our efforts as writers.

My experience has taught me that writing is a divine art form, one to which we all have access and at which we all have the innate ability to succeed. And when we return to that most natural of all states, it comes easily, smoothly and quickly for all of us, including those who have been blocked for decades. Simply by doing the right things to ease one's way through the block and then reconnecting with the divine inspiration, to which we all have access on the other side, the words flow out easily, smoothly, and inspirationally.

I have seen this transpire thousands of times in my retreats and classes. And this would not have been the case had writing not already been a natural art form available to all of us. For each and every time I helped my students remove their innocently self-imposed blocks and to reconnect to God through their writing, they did just that. And that would not have been possible had they not already established a place to land. That place, of course, was on the runway of their personal path of divinely-inspired writing.

Envy appears when you go there, while someone else feels that they cannot get there himself; or from those others, who cannot believe that they even have such a personal, divinely-ordained path available to them.

Rather than studying the successful routes of others, most envious people choose to put down the brave individual for taking those first steps. The envious individual is scared, as noted above, of her own success.

So, what do you do?

Should you cave in to the pressures and opinions of others? Would that benefit anyone?

Crawling back into the shadows that once loomed over you benefits no one.

This concept is best covered in a renowned passage from the book *A Return to Love: Reflections on the Principles of "A Course in Miracles,"* written by bestselling author Marianne Williamson.

Our deepest fear is not that we are inadequate.
Our deepest fear is that we are powerful beyond measure.
It is our light, not our darkness
That most frightens us. (Williamson 1992)

Stay with Ms. Williamson's words for a moment longer. Read them over a time or two again. Breathe them in. And then do that again and again. You may even want to make it a part of your daily preparatory routine to read over and really absorb the essence of Ms. Williamson's full poem every morning. I know I do and doing so has significantly enhanced my life.

So, what can you do about those who react enviously to your steps forward on your inspirational path?

Love them! That's right, love them!

For in essence, they are doing you an extreme favor by bringing to your attention, through the projection of their fears onto you, exactly what it is that is keeping you from stepping into the full you.

"Remove the illusions, lift the veils, and you will rest in the heart. Rest in the heart, and God will abide with you.
PAUL FERRINI;
Reflections of the Christ Mind

"Not to be able to stop thinking is a dreadful addiction, but we don't realize this because almost everyone is suffering from it, so it is considered normal."
ECKHART TOLLE
The Power of Now

You have healed yourself of those wounds on a soul level. There will no longer be a reason for them to mirror back to you your former fears, because they are gone. And as a result, either the projection, and the need for it, will disappear, or the person who was doing the mirroring back to you will disappear from your life.

There's an old saying by Erma Bombeck: "A child needs your love most when he deserves it least."

For like everyone, and as dismal as it may appear at times, they are simply doing the best that they can. How can you fault someone for doing the best that they can?

And how do you love them?

You love them by accepting them for who they are right here and right now, rather than expecting them to be something that they are not. And here's the greatest personal gift that will come to you from loving them—when you love them, unappealing characteristics and all, you are really loving yourself. For we are all mirrors for each other.

Have you ever noticed that when you've had a conflict with someone else and you finally just gave in, that the other person seemed to do the same?

Loving certain characteristics in others that we find unappealing, offers us the opportunity to love those same characteristics or wounds within ourselves. Once we dip into feeling a sensitivity and compassion for another, we are really feeling that same compassion and sensitivity for ourselves. It is then that the healing of ourselves by ourselves transpires, which is what life is all about. The more healing that takes place, the more room is freed within us and in each of our lives for the Spirit to inhabit, and the greater impact we each will have during our time on the planet.

You know as well as I that real love is not a result of some sort of bargain. It is not, "I will love you, if you will love me."

Real love, the divine love that you are experiencing and furthering in your life, expects nothing in return. It just is and seeks to be expressed and shared. Real love sets out to find a home in the hearts of others, no matter how hard those hearts may be.

Did you ever notice that the person who dislikes dogs or cats the most is also the one to whom those animals seem uncontrollably drawn? Because that person needs the love of those divine beings more than anyone else. And all they want to do is to share what comes so naturally to them, especially with those who need it most.

So, how do you love those who attack you with envy or jealousy?

Let me reply to that question with another question: What is the one thing you can give to another, and possibly to the world, that no one else can?

Yourself.

So how do you love another by just being you—yes, you—and not the someone they supposedly want you to be? Don't expect anything from them, especially initially. Then, ruthlessly, and with reckless abandon, just be who you are. Being who you are helps them grow more and more comfortable with who they are. Or, if they're not willing to go there, they'll eventually learn to just leave you alone. The anger they toss at you, when not absorbed by you, returns to them. And, at least, they will stop being so downtrodden. Because, with you no longer taking out their emotional garbage for them, they will end up having to do so themselves. Then, they will finally begin to catch a whiff of the stink that they've been casting out for years. Only after their pain reaches this level, will they finally be willing to learn from your example and reconnect to their divine times, or find a way to change on their own.

"[To] thine own self be true. . ." - William Shakespeare, *Hamlet* (I.iii.79).

It's time to quit using others as an excuse for you not being you. For in reality, in their own desperate way, these blessed souls are trying to challenge you to bring out the real you in the only way they know how.

For a greater perspective and a faster path through this necessary transformation in your life, I suggest you read and do the exercises in my book, *Write to Heal.*

Chapter Six
Enlightenment

So, am I saying that, out of all of the many benefits available to you through the writing of your book, that possibly the greatest is to reach enlightenment? And that possibly, even beside all of the other reasons, that's the primary reason you as a human being have been drawn to author a book or books?

Yes, unequivocally, that is what I am saying.

This, of course, now brings us to the topic of the bright pink elephant sitting right smack in the middle of the room, and of course leads us to the really big question: What is enlightenment?

For you to move any further into the reading of this book and further into the progression that is available to you through the writing of your book(s), it is only fair that you get an in-depth and accurate response to that question. For, in reality, the opportunity to acquire heightened enlightenment quickly is really what this whole book is about, is it not? But before we move any further into this process, you deserve to know not only what enlightenment is, but also toward what form of enlightenment the writing of your books(s) will lead you.

According to the *Random House College Dictionary*, the one my mother got me before I took off for college, the root word of "enlightenment," or "enlighten," is defined as "to give intellectual or spiritual light to; to instruct, impart knowledge to."

Of course, especially in the New Age world of today, oftentimes enlightenment, the type that the Buddha, Christ, and Mohammed supposedly experienced, is what

"Through surrender, spiritual energy comes into the world."
ECKHART TOLLE
The Power of Now

"The transformation of your world will depend on your remembering."
NEALE DONALD WALSCH;
Communion with God

enlightenment is thought to be. And people are referred to as either enlightened or not.

As a result, a person is either seen as enlightened, one with God and beyond this world we live in, or not.

However, in reality, in one way or another and at one time or another, we are all enlightened. You know what I mean: the moment or instance when we act or speak with the type of love and compassion we would attribute to a benevolent Almighty.

What we all really seek is not so much enlightenment. For we are all, with the exception of an extremely wayward few in our culture, already enlightened—at least some of the time. Even Hannibal Lecter had his good side. His bad side was just so hideous that it overwhelmed his enlightened side.

So, the good news is that you are already enlightened. You already have the direct connection to the Almighty that makes your light go on. What you need to do is just adjust the cord a little bit, so that your connection better slips into your power source. With that connection in place, not only will your light shine more brightly, but also more consistently for longer periods of time. You will become more and more enlightened; for light attracts light.

And the writing of your book, if pursued through the proper approach, can definitely do that for you. For remember, as mentioned already in the Introduction, it says in the most prominently placed sentence in the New Testament, John 1:1, "In the beginning was the Word, and the Word was with God, and the Word was God."

But before we go any further, let's get real about this topic. For even Christ, the Buddha, and Muhammed experienced having the cords fall out of their outlets every once in awhile. They became real humans. The biggest difference between them and those around them was that they knew when the cord fell out or partially wiggled free from the outlet. And they were smart enough to take the time to disappear into the wilderness, just as Christ did, to push that cord back in.

Writing your book, through the method I have been born to share, will not only make your light shine brightly and consistently, but the process of doing so will also make you aware of when your cord has loosened itself away from the outlet.

It will also offer you a route to get yourself immediately plugged back in, so that any necessary healing, and thus enlightenment, can begin.

For the best and most realistic understanding of enlightenment, here are a few other important points to keep in mind.

First, enlightenment is progressive.

Fifteen years ago, as an adult, I found the home that I had always been looking for since my childhood. Or should I say it found me? Fifteen years ago, mystical, magical Sedona, Arizona reached out and drew me to her.

As you probably know, Sedona is known as the spiritual Mecca of not only North America, but possibly the world. All types of spiritually aware individuals are drawn to her. Many who feel the pull to Sedona expect a miracle anointing of sorts to result from their relocation. More than a few proclaim themselves as the next great messiah.

As they leave their former lives behind, these individuals idealistically expect that all of the dysfunctions they have created—the broken relationships, the abuse, the poverty, and all of the other areas where they sold themselves way too short—will just fall away as they cross into Sedona.

MAE WEST: "For a long time I was ashamed of the way I lived." Did you reform?
MAE WEST: "No, I'm not ashamed anymore."

"If error is corrected whenever it is recognized as such, the path of error is the path of truth."

HANS
REICHENBACH

43

There is no doubt that Sedona carries with her a much higher spiritual energy level than do other locales. As a result, their dysfunctions, which have not been left behind as they originally thought, are not defused at all. Instead, those dysfunctions are spiritually exaggerated by their move to Sedona.

Instead of being anointed as the next Buddha, Mohammed, or Christ, upon entering Sedona, their dysfunctions, which in reality represent huge opportunities for personal growth and advancement, flare up. Their lives go tumbling downward, farther and farther and farther down, until the pain becomes so great that they have to change.

Most don't make it that far before they go running out of town, as if their hair were on fire.

The point I am trying to make is that enlightenment is a progression. And even though it appears completely out of the blue to the casual observer, nothing could be further from the truth. For enlightenment comes in steps and stages.

Even in Christ's case, the divine timing, in which he finally became and began living the life of "The Christ," didn't culminate until he was around thirty years old, and had progressively gone through all of the stuff and steps leading to that transformation.

The same can be said for Gandhi and Mohammed. How about the Buddha? How did he go through that long of progression of steps to become "The Buddha"? That, of course, didn't mean that he was not enlightened before that moment. It just meant that he became a whole lot more enlightened after he passed through that doorway where his real spirit and identity became known, not only to others, but mainly to himself.

Even J. Gordon Liddy, the great present-day Christian author and spokesperson, went through a massive number of steps to become the inspired beacon he is today.

So, again, the point I am trying to make is that whatever level of enlightenment we seek (and are ready for) is progressive. Even if you aspire to be the next great messiah, it will still happen in stages until that spotlight of yours comes on for good.

Writing your book through a divinely-led method can and will offer an opportunity for a greater degree of enlightenment. I have never seen that not be the case with anyone who has properly applied the method I share.

Plugging directly into that spiritual, inspirational outlet to the Almighty, that we all possess, will bring amazing things.

It offers us direct access to God incarnate, the pure, white light of the universe.

Then, as we remain connected to that ultimate source, that light pours into and through us during the entire time we are writing our books. As we write, that white light blazes a path through our bodies, minds, emotions, healing wounds, and turning up the light that shines through us several notches.

Thus, we don't become enlightened. Even the powerful tool of writing cannot create something that didn't already exist. We become more enlightened, way more enlightened as years of worry, doubts, concerns, frustrations, and fears are swept out of us—poof—gone for good.

As that baggage is released, room is cleared for the white light of the Almighty to fill that space, formerly inhabited by our wounds and bruises. As a result, we take a huge leap forward. Oftentimes, decades of pain are healed and the massive spaces they used to fill in our lives are replaced by the white light of the Almighty. We become not enlightened, but instead, more enlightened.

The second major point that I want to make about enlightenment is that what is possible varies from person to person.

Simply put, the amount of enlightenment that a person can step up to is directly determined by the amount of white light one can handle, or is willing to take on, and that is determined by a variety of factors, including diet, fitness level, general openness, the amount of karma a person is carrying, or the specific phase in one's life, just to mention a few.

Oftentimes I find that the amount of enlightenment that individuals will experience as the result of writing their books is dependent upon whether they are old or new souls.

What type of enlightenment can you expect as the result of writing your book through the spirit-led manner that I propose?

Again, even though the enlightenment one experiences from writing will always appear significant, making this major leap forward, as you will see in the next chapter, still varies from person to person.

Chapter Seven

What Does the Enlightenment One Experiences Through Writing a Book Lead To?

Many years ago, as part of my own spiritual development, I struggled miserably with a variety of issues that were causing me intense emotional pain.

Despite the fact that I am very physical, I am even more of an emotional being. So if I am going to feel pain, at least initially, it surfaces in an emotional fashion. As a result, I experience intense, immense emotional pain, which oftentimes then manifests physically. However, in this one particular incident, my pain had not yet transferred to a physical level.

Being in as much pain as I was, I needed help, so I sought the assistance of my friend, Gordon Stonehouse, who, in his typically calm manner, shared with me, as simplistic as it sounded at the time, exactly what I needed to hear.

"Pain is nothing more and nothing less than resistance to growth," Gordon told me.

When Gordon shared his explanation with me, even as a result of my own state of denial, it completely resonated as truth. And I must admit that I have spent the last thirty years testing his theory and have consistently found what Gordon shared with me to be true.

As you will see from the following vignettes, the forms into which people choose to channel their resistance vary greatly. Even though everyone has a primary way in which they feel pain, all persons mix and match their pain in a variety of manners. For some, resistance manifests as

"To the dull mind all of nature is leaden. To the illumined mind the whole world sparkles with light."

EMERSON

"Our doubts are traitors, and make us lose the good we oft might win by fearing to attempt."

SHAKESPEARE

"He partitioned off twenty cubits at the rear of the temple with cedar boards from the floor to the ceiling to form within the temple an inner sanctuary, the Most Holy Place."

I KINGS 6:16

"It is not necessary to seek God because God is already the essence of who you are. To connect with God, simply remove all judgments and thoughts that do not bless you and others."

PAUL FERRINI;
Reflections of the Christ Mind

physical pain. Others numb the pain through overworking, having too many responsibilities or whatever, and don't even feel it until they finally slow down and it catches up with them. Others bury their pain, like a dog buries a bone, and plan to come back when the time and need for the bone is right.

What does all of this have to do with writing—or enlightenment?

Enlightenment is basically a large step forward, as a result of both personal and spiritual growth, beyond what has been holding one back. As I explained earlier, what has typically been holding one back is commonly referred to as karma, which lies on the other side of enlightenment.

What does all this have to do with the writing of a book?

When an author connects with her book, through the method described in my other books, that person also connects, for an extensive period of time, directly with the Oneness of God. When that connection happens, and the person stays connected for a significant amount of time, the healing, loving White Light of God really has a chance to go to work, cleaning out the karma that is no longer needed, to make a permanent space for itself. The natural by-product of this all-important transition is enlightenment.

Where then does the pain come in during this essential process?

Any pain, physical or otherwise, that we feel during this process is nothing more and nothing less than our own resistance to our eventual enlightenment and growth.

As you will see from the following, each of the persons featured, as the result of writing their books according to the method that I refer to, intimately experienced their own way of dealing with their resistance-centered pain.

As you will see, some buried their pain. Others desensitized themselves to it, while still others manifested their pain physically or emotionally. Either way, each one came to terms with their own resistance through the writing of their books, and a deeper sense of enlightenment transpired.

Why do I tell you this and why do I share this with you?

Because I want to introduce you to the myriad of ways and means through which your own resistance will surface during the writing of your book. That way, you will be emotionally prepared in advance to deal with it. Then, when it surfaces, you will allow yourself to ease through it, instead of falling into shock and thus becoming stunned. If you became stunned, you would likely halt the writing of your book, as opposed to flowing with it. This would impede the steps of the enlightenment process laid out for you.

As verification of a direct connection with an all-healing process, I have included a collection of vignettes, that I feel capture the scope and breadth of what you can expect to experience through the writing of your book when employing my suggested method.

To protect the privacy of the individuals, whose stories follow, I have changed names and varied their descriptions. With that in mind, I can guarantee you that these stories are all true. They are also a small sampling of thousands. You will also see that they cover a gamut of big, enlightening steps forward, which, through the healing of relationships, misconceptions, and long-festering wounds, we are used to seeing in those who come to us for assistance in the writing of their books.

As you will also see from these personal accounts, the awe-inspiring enlightenment available to you through the

"Whether you think you can, or that you can't, you are usually right."
HENRY FORD

"He made righteousness readable."
JAMES BONE

writing of books takes a few different versions, or can be received as a mixing and matching of possible outcomes. The enlightenment you will receive can most obviously surface as:

A physical healing, perhaps connected to the discovery of a past wrong committed by or against you, with an attempt to correct the ensuing damage created,

All of which lead to. . .

A much-needed, significantly revised relationship with yourself, and greater personal clarity surrounding your true identity and your true purpose as a human being.

Any of these possibilities will lead to opportunities for a remarkably enhanced life through the living of one's soul purpose. In most cases, our soul purpose has been trying to burn its way through to us, by removing the blocks in our lives. All of these lead us to our right to divine peace in our lives, a peace sought by us all.

If you like what you read below and would like to hear more stories, feel free to visit my website www.tom.bird.com, where hundreds of video testimonials await you.

Chris - Enlightenment Through the Direct Discovery of One's Life Purpose

Chris, a man in his early forties, came to us as the result of a recommendation by one of our authors, who had already taken a retreat and completed her book. Thus, Chris was already familiar with our technique.

Upon first glance, you would say that Chris had everything a person would want. He was tall, handsome, fit, happily married, well-respected professionally, supported emotionally by his family, and in the top 1 percent of income earners in the country. He was also very intelligent; bright enough to understand that there was something missing in his life. He may not have known exactly what was missing, but he knew that his soul was searching for something. Despite how drawn Chris was to write, I didn't get the impression that he thought he would find whatever his soul was looking for by writing a book at one of our retreats. But that was exactly what transpired.

In my exchanges with Chris, I received the impression that he was an all-or-nothing guy. If he were going to commit to an undertaking, he was going to suspend any and all disbelief, or whatever else could hold him back, and give his all to that endeavor. That was exactly what he came prepared to do at our retreat. And he arrived super-prepared. He had read all of the books we suggested, watched all of the videos, and done all of the pre-retreat writing assignments. So, Chris came to the retreat more than prepared to succeed. As a result, he finished writing his book on the very first day of the retreat.

It was then—not during the writing of his book, and not in preparation to do so—that Chris caved emotionally. All of a sudden he became very distraught, confused, and desperate for help. He came to me, expressing a desire to see the life coach I had staffing the retreat. As our Author Within Coach, she was responsible for the emotional preparation of our attendees at the retreat and to usher them through their spiritual and psychological transitions.

With multiple degrees, certifications, and talents at her disposal, she was caring and compassionate about her

"A heav'n on earth."
JOHN MILTON

"Readers are of two sorts; one who carefully goes through a book, and the other who as carefully lets the book go through him."
DOUGLAS JERROLD

RICKY RICARDO:
"There you go again, wanting something that you haven't got."
LUCY RICARDO: *"I do not, I just want to see what I haven't got that I don't want."*
I LOVE LUCY

work with our authors, and her presence was a welcome addition at our retreats.

"Life is like an overlong drama through which we sit being nagged by the vague memories of having read the reviews."
JOHN UPDIKE

When an attendee approaches our life coach at a retreat to raise a question or concern, she responds immediately by taking that individual aside, and establishing a very private, caring space for them to receive whatever attention they both need and deserve.

When Chris asked to meet with our life coach, I immediately escorted him over to her. Unfortunately for Chris, our life coach was already in-session with another author. Seeing that he was visibly shaken, I decided to wait with him. As he sat there and we started to talk, Chris began to share his story with me.

Chris had had a dream since he was very young, one that he pursued with vigor as soon as he came of age to do so. He felt called to be an astronaut. But grow as he did, Chris eventually found himself too tall to be an astronaut. Instead, he went into aeronautical engineering, where he became very successful and where he was able to create a safe and secure life for his family. Yet, inside of himself he could see, through writing his book at the retreat, that he was still reaching for the stars and that writing could get him there.

Right then and there, Chris realized that the path to the stars he had been waiting for had been presented to him by writing a book. Right then and there, he was ready to make the necessary changes in his lifestyle. But he was concerned that he would lose his wife, whom he felt just wouldn't understand. And he feared ruining the life of the young daughter he loved so much.

"You can convert your style into riches."
QUENTIN CRISP

More than anything else, right at that divine moment, Chris understood that, after he had been unable to realize his dream of becoming an astronaut due to his height, he had instead built a life around what his head wanted, as

opposed to his heart. Now, he was willing to chuck it all for the place where his heart was leading him.

This awe-inspiring understanding represented a dream found, which was not unlike what numerous life-changing leaders experience before aligning themselves with their life missions. Chris's realization in that moment led him not only to complete the revision of his book and to get it published, but also to make all of the necessary changes in his life to live his divine purpose as a writer. At the time of this writing, the book he wrote at his retreat was only weeks away from being published and distributed worldwide. And for all intents and purposes, he was only months away from seeing his heartfelt efforts find a home on a best seller list.

Vivian - Enlightenment Through the Removal of a Temporary Physical Barrier

As Deepak Chopra and many other teachers have shown, there is definitely a distinct, even direct, and unadulterated connection between the mind and the body.

So, what does the mind do when it becomes overly-concerned about a particular perspective, while venturing into the writing of a book? The mind creates or exaggerates an injury in the body. So frequent is this occurrence, that I don't remember the last time we hosted a retreat where at least one attendee was not suffering from some sort of writing-obstructive ailment.

"Beneath the rule of men entirely great, the pen is mightier than the sword."
EDWARD BULWER
LYTTON

Such was the case with Vivian, a talented young woman with a tremendous upside, whose shoulder on her writing arm began to ache uncontrollably, almost out of the blue, when she started to pen her book. As a result of her pain she also became irritable. So when I tried to explain that the pain she was feeling was just her own resistance manifesting physically, neither my comments, nor my suggestions on how to alleviate her pain were met with open arms.

Finally, as frequently ends up being the case, during my fourth talk with her on the subject, with each of our prior three discussions rising in intensity, I just told her the truth, this time, more directly and with a little more power.

"Listen," I said, "you can just give into the pain and walk out of this room right now. But if you do, you will be giving into the self-imposed pain and you will never finish your book.

"I told you everything you need to know to get through it," I continued. "You can breathe your way through it, write your way through it, or you can just give up and walk out right now. It's up to you what you choose to do. I have given you my best advice."

Sometimes, thank God, though not often, a person's resistance is so great in order to open the way for the Creator-led Inspiration, that comes through the writing of a book. And the writer is so used to resisting, that her resistance, embodied for so long, just needs to be met with a greater force. I provided Vivian with that greater force when I read her the riot act.

Ultimately, her fear of failing by not finishing her book was even greater than her resistance to doing so. Within a few minutes, she was writing up a storm—pain free. Within the hour, her book was completed.

The pain. Where did it go? It left with her resistance; and she was amazed.

But often our resistance surfaces most strongly when the Spirit-led inspiration that comes with the writing of our book is just about to break through for good.

The result?

Enlightenment.

Specifically in this case, Vivian elevated herself to a whole new level in her life. An aspiring songwriter and vocalist, she was able to transfer what she learned through the writing of her book to the creation of lyrics. Her singing took off, as well. Last we heard, she was on a whole new track, much of which resulted from the breakthrough she experienced while writing her book.

Beth - Enlightenment By First Healing One's Self, which Leads to the Healing of Relationships with Loved Ones

Beth was a retired school administrator—determined, but angry and judgmental. Accustomed to absolute control and doing things her way, she had deliberately decided to skirt a few of the suggestions I had in place for the retreat. I was unaware of this until her cell phone began ringing during her retreat, in the middle of a Sunday morning writing session. It was Mother's Day.

Beth could see by the expression on my face that I was none too happy.

However, as if she were expecting it to ring for some good reason, she struck a very apologetic pose as she rose from her chair, cell phone in hand, and quickly scurried from the room.

After a few minutes, Beth, tears in her eyes, motioned me outside of the retreat room to speak with her. The hardness of her expression and disposition had all disappeared by then. She sobbed as she began by

"Were you to see only that spark of light within yourself and others, all perception of darkness in your experience would dissolve."
PAUL FERRINI;
Reflections of the Christ Mind

"For me a picture should be something likeable, joyous and pretty...yes pretty. There are enough ugly things in life for us not to add them."
PIERRE AUGUSTE RENOIR

apologizing for leaving her cell phone on and taking the call during retreat time.

"It was my son," she said, still crying. "He has refused speak to me for the last four years and today he broke the ice to call and wish me a happy Mother's Day."

Beth paused for a moment to wipe the tears from her eyes before continuing.

"You know what's amazing, Tom?" she asked. "His call came in at just the exact moment when, as part of my book, I was finishing up a letter to him, where I was asking him to forgive me for riding him so hard.

"It just seemed like when I finally admitted my wrongdoing as a parent, asked for his forgiveness through my writing, and in doing so, actually forgave myself, as well, that he called."

"I can see how the two are connected, Tom. I truly can. Now, it appears as if I have my son back and I think it's because of the writing of my book. And now that I know the truth about the mistakes I made with him, I will make sure to never make those same mistakes again."

Nancy - Enlightenment Through the Uncovering of a Previously Unknown Situation or Fact

Nancy wanted to write in the worst way. She knew she wanted to write, but she had no idea what it was that she was going to write. But she just felt drawn to write more and more each day. Her deep desire to do so, coupled with her desperation at not knowing how to go about doing so, is what drove her to my retreat. When she finally sat down to write, words started spilling out of her, like water out of a garden hose on high. As a result, she was drawn into a very deep, almost obsessive, connection with that which came pouring out of her.

Nancy was in her late forties, a time when hidden understandings often come to those whose physical strength has depleted just enough. What they have been subconsciously hiding for so long can finally begin powering its way into their consciousness.

The book that Nancy wrote focused on how she had been sexually abused by an assortment of men from age nine until well into her adolescent years. Until that time, she had been unaware of this past trauma. This was something she had not been aware of up until that time. Before then, the realization of her situation would have scarred her psyche for life. That realization chose to emerge many years after she had reached the safe haven of a strong marriage with a really great husband.

As Nancy wrote, and then re-read, the book she wrote in the retreat, for the first time in her life so many things finally began to make sense. As a result, her healing from the abuse was almost instantaneous.

Even while she was still living with her husband in the small midwestern town where the abuse took place, Nancy went on to publish her book, which was instrumental in her healing process.

Today, having let go of the confining, subconscious presence of her past, Nancy couldn't be happier and more at peace, a place where she admits she wouldn't have arrived without writing her book.

Natalie - Enlightenment Through the Preparation Afforded by a Premonition

"Some call it evolution and others call it God."
WILLIAM H. CARRUTH

Natalie was a mere fourteen years old when she attended her first retreat. Like her older co-participants, she had no idea what she was going to write during the retreat, but she had no doubt in her mind that she wanted to write a book. What she did write about changed her life for the better.

Natalie wrote a novel based upon her buried feelings regarding the abuse inflicted by her alcoholic father upon her, her younger brother, and especially the physical and emotional abuse she witnessed her mother endure.

In her book's final scene, Natalie's young protagonist, easily recognizable as the young author herself, sits beside her father's hospital bed, as he lay dying from the effects of his alcoholic habits. In the scene, her father tries to right all of his wrongs by apologizing to her before passing.

Natalie went on to get her book published, but not before her father did indeed pass in his sleep from an alcohol-induced heart attack. He never apologized; he never even made an attempt to do so. But the writing of her book helped Natalie prepare and move beyond the pain her father brought upon her and her family, and to have the peace she finally deserved from his passing.

Some believe that part of Natalie's ability to acquire the peace we all seek resulted from her father's apology. Even though he was unable to offer her his apology in person during his life, it came through so strongly in the book, which she was able to complete prior to his passing.

Through writing her book, Natalie was able to look at the pain of her past, release it, and heal. Today, she is a happy, confident, and successful young woman.

Barbara - Enlightenment Through the Healing of a Long-Term Ailment or Illness

Barbara was a highly-successful professional with the personality of an obsessive perfectionist. As successful as she was, to get to the next level, she had to get her name out there more prominently. She chose to write and publish a book as her chosen method to do so.

Unfortunately, she had severely damaged her right shoulder in a car accident a few years before, and this injury had affected her dominant right hand. Even though her shoulder checked out fine according to her doctor, it still caused her a significant amount of pain. Barbara was concerned that the pain and discomfort would prevent her from writing her book longhand at her retreat.

However, every time she brought up her concern to me before the retreat, I just kept getting the intuitive message to share with Barbara that, despite her concerns, everything would be fine with her shoulder, and for her to just show up at the retreat. She did.

But everything was not fine when she showed up at the retreat. In fact, Barbara forced herself to write through excruciating shoulder pain for the first several hours, until finally she came to the point where she had to choose between continuing to write her book or to leave. This all climaxed at a time when it became apparent that, for her book to blossom, just writing the facts and figures she wanted to share wouldn't be enough. She would actually have to share her soul by releasing what I refer to as her "author's voice." When I explained this to Barbara, she started to cry. Doing so had been something that she had been avoiding in every area of her life for potentially her entire life.

When I told her that, Barbara, the perfectionist who refused to let herself fail, immediately went back to her writing, now more determined than ever. And with that step now taken, not only was her unique voice birthed on paper, but her longtime shoulder pain left forever.

With her author's voice leading the way, Barbara not only completed the writing of her first book at her retreat, but has gone on to write two others, as well.

"Every situation – nay, every moment – is of infinite worth; for it is the representative of a whole eternity."
GOETHE

"Better to write for yourself and have no public, than write for the public and have no self."
CYRIL CONNOLLY

You see, often physical pain or other types of resistance are misunderstood as blockages, when in reality, they are directional in nature. They point us in the direction we need to go to take our next step on the road to our own eventual pot of gold at the end of the rainbow. This is available to us all, both through the actual process of writing, but also, and especially, the completion of our Spirit-led books.

Chapter Eight

When God Comes Calling Through an Obsessive Desire to Write a Book, He/She/It Really Comes Calling

As you will see from the vignettes on the life styles of a few earthshaking writers just before they struck it big, the obsessive draw to write, when combined with its relentless tie to divine timing can become all-consuming. Everything else is pushed out of the way to let the God-connection of writing come streaming through. Possibly, in one way or another, you can relate to the stories which follow. Of course, each of the following cases are real, but extreme, which I believe is reflective of how far God will go, when the time is right, to get our attention.

The key to avoiding the type of temporary deprivation associated with the world-renowned authors described below, is to start listening to and acting upon the signs in your life related to divine timing. And to start listening a lot earlier than they did. That is possibly why you are reading this book now. That way, you won't have to give up so much to do so much with your writing.

Either way though, one thing is for sure: By making this connection through your book, your life, and potentially the lives of millions of others, will forever be altered and changed for the better.

"Wisdom entereth not into a malicious mind."
RABELAIS

"An optimist may see a light where there is none. But must the pessimist always run to blow it out?"
MICHAEL de SAINT-PIERRE

Tom Bird

Rubin "Hurricane" Carter

Rubin "Hurricane" Carter was a world-class boxer in the '70s, known for his brutal approach to the sport. He was as far away from being an author as anyone could imagine.

However, after being wrongly convicted on a trumped-up murder charge, Carter was sent to prison. There, for the first time in his life, he felt called and began to write.

The release of his book, *The Sixteenth Round: From Number 1 Contender to Number 45472,* which he finished in prison, took the country by storm, and led to a major movement by an entire generation to get Carter released from prison.

Carter's book changed the lives of many and significantly altered how Americans would view inmates from that point forward.

As professional of a boxer as Carter was, he will always be best remembered for the author he became while in prison.

J.K. Rowling

Rowling was an inexperienced, aspiring author and single mom, who had fallen on hard times and had begun living on the streets with her son. Her life had been reduced to the point where she had nothing to do but write, which was all she wanted to do anyway. By obsessively taking to her writing, the only thing that seemed to be working in her life, Rowling was following the personal call of her soul.

"All good writing is swimming underwater and holding your breath."

F. SCOTT FITZGERALD

"After a time, you may find that having is not so pleasing a thing, after all, as wanting. It is not logical, but it is often true."

SPOCK, STAR TREK

Her first book, *Harry Potter and the Sorcerer's Stone*, written during that tough time, was an instant best seller. Not only have seven of Rowling's books been made into movies, but she is the bestselling author of all time in England, with over 350 million books sold worldwide.

Sylvester Stallone

Like Rollins and Carter, Sylvester Stallone's life had been reduced to the bare minimum, living on the streets, bunking occasionally at a friend's house, and writing. Of course, he was writing a screenplay, which mimicked a version of his own comeback tale. But like the others, the writing bug had definitely bitten him. In fact, it had bitten him so hard that he could do little else, which was partially the reason for his reduced life style, proving that when divine timing steps up to the plate, it really steps up to the plate. And when God comes calling, He/She/It really comes-a-calling.

Of course, as a result of Sly's devotion during this time, not only did he strike it big with his Rocky series, but as a world-changing actor, as well.

Neale Donald Walsch

Speak of when God comes-a-calling—He/She/It really comes-a-calling through an obsessive desire to write and relentless divine timing.

Of course, Walsch's story is well-known. Due to a combination of circumstances, Walsch, too, had become homeless, and wrote the first book in his Conversations with God series while living in the indigent section of a public campground in Oregon.

"There are hazards in anything one does, but there are greater hazards in doing nothing."
SHIRLEY WILLIAMS

"When the individual starts for the Promised Land, the land of darkness must be forsaken, forgotten."
BAIRD T SPALDING;
Life and Teaching of the Masters of the Far East

As with the others listed above, Walsch's life had been reduced to ruins so that not only did he have the time to write, but writing was the only thing he could do.

Of course, in what could possibly be the case with you and your book, as well, Walsch improved tens of millions of lives when he finally gave in to the writing and publishing of his books.

How can you begin tapping into and connecting with this divine timing, as it is speaking to you through your life? Employ the methodology for writing laid out later in this book, ask questions, and write… Write right now.

Chapter Nine

Books Can Be Relentless About Getting Their Messages Through, Not Only to You, But Out to the World, As Well

If you are anything like those who have attended my classes and retreats over the last three decades, your book(s) have probably visited you relentlessly, waking you up in the middle of the night, taking the form of an inspiration during a long car drive or during other relaxing occasions, or when it literally just came pouring through you onto paper or onto a screen. Just as relentless as it may have been in getting your attention, it will be just as relentless, if not more so, to get out into the world.

In that way, it will act out like a literary child. Seeing it from that perspective will be a great help to you. Like kids, a book may be born through us, but it has his or her life purpose. And just like you, it will never give up and it will be relentless in pursuit of its goals. Because we have now entered into, thank God, The Golden Age of Book Publishing, your book will now have more options than ever before to get itself out to the world, not in years, but right now. And it will be taking you with it. For it is you who will be receiving all of the earthly credit due for creating it, when in reality you were only responsible for its essential release.

So watch out. Birthing your book through you comprises just the beginning of your marvelous relationship with this divine inspiration and creation.

Because it will want to reach as many people, directly or indirectly, as possible. And like raising children, you can both be part of their process and become a part of where they

MR. SPOCK: "May I point out that I had an opportunity to observe your counterparts quite closely. They were brutal, savage, unprincipled, uncivilized, treacherous – in every way, splendid examples of Homo Sapiens. The very flower of humanity. I found them quite refreshing."
CAPTAIN KIRK (to Dr. McCoy): "I'm not sure, but I think we've been insulted."

STAR TREK

"O ye Gods grant us what is good whether we pray for it or not, but keep evil from us even though we pray for it."

PLATO

"I have seen you in the sanctuary and beheld your power and your glory."

PSALM 63:2

"You have to leave the city of your comfort and go into the wilderness of your intuition. What you'll discover will be wonderful. What you'll discover will be yourself."

ALAN ALDA

"To see a world in a grain of sand and heaven in a wild flower, to hold infinity in the palm of your hand and eternity in an hour."

WILLIAM BLAKE

are going, or they will run you over and you can pick up the pieces later.

Further, if you are anything like the new brand of authors I see coming through my retreats, the book seeking to be birthed through you is, by all probability, a trendsetter. The inspiration of God, as it comes through you in the form of a book, wants to change the world, not merely leave it the same. It wants to make a difference. So when writing your book, using the method I describe in my other books, you can expect to pen a life-changing work. Conventional publishers, by nature, are trend followers. See the natural conflict there? This is one of the many reasons I suggest avoiding them at all costs (see my book, *Write to Publish*).

But no matter how blind they may be, the message confined in your book will find its way. And as long you don't impede the process, you will, again, end up getting all of the credit for the dramatic effects of your life-changing book. In some ways, this doesn't seem fair. But in reality, I don't really feel that your book cares very much about receiving any credit. For all it wants is to get its message delivered, even if that message is responsible for nothing more than making someone smile or laugh.

To give you an idea of just how great the staying power of your book will be in finding its audience, I have included some short vignettes below on authors whose names you will recognize. Like you, they were led by the spirit of their books to write. Like you probably are, they were trendsetters. So their roads to publication and to their audiences were not easy rows to hoe. They had to pass through the conservative peepholes of the conventional publishing world, which at the time controlled what and who was published. With the fall of the economy, much has changed for the better. Conventional publishers no longer unfairly rule the roost. Instead, as it should be, you and your book are now in charge of your collective literary fates.

Just to prove the point, though, about how collectively obsessive and committed an author and book tandem can be, I have chosen to share the following vignettes. Despite the fact that the restraining factors you will be dealing with as an author are far, far less in numbers and power than the ones these legendary authors had to deal with, you can still expect the popularity of your book to take a number of twists and turns, en route to living its purpose. That purpose, that desire to get its message delivered can come in many forms, as well. It can directly reach millions, like most best sellers. Or, it can directly affect the lives of a small number of prominent voices, who can then carry its message to the masses. Or, like Paul's dealings with the stranger on the road to Damascus, it can directly affect just one person, who, fueled by its message, can directly affect not only the world, but the world for centuries to come.

In the following vignettes, I believe you will find many a hidden and obvious message meant just for you, as your own personal, divinely-led authors lead to each and every one of the following. So, I recommend that you read each of the following very slowly, while paying attention to which authors' experiences speak to you and how.

The following author stories are meant as inspirational accounts of the successes of many writers, who sought (and in these cases, achieved) literary notoriety by stubbornly following their inward callings. Several of these stories tell the tale of well-known writers, many of whom sit atop the literary canon.

"Little Lamb who made thee? Dost thou know who made thee?"
WILLIAM BLAKE

"It is hard to fight an enemy who has outposts in your head."
SALLY KEMPTON

"Mistakes are the portals of discovery."
JAMES JOYCE

Though icons of literature now, their personal stories reflect a long period of failure and disappointment before persevering and eventually finding their "big shot." Subsequently, a few of the stories show that the publishing world has changed dramatically in recent years. Gone are the days of an elite few publishing houses, refusing to publish lesser known works or "no name" writers. On the contrary, many authors self-publish or find their way into the publishing market through smaller publishing companies.

As well, I suggest, that as you begin on your own journey, that you stay open and flexible, as you and your book move onto the stage of publication, where the ride can become unexpected and exciting, if you just let it be so.

Jane Austen

Easily one of the greatest writers in the history of the English language, Jane Austen wrote her masterpiece *First Impressions* in 1797. Initially deemed unworthy of being read, that slight actually may have contributed directly to the book's eventual literary greatness. For Austen revised and then re-titled the book *Pride and Prejudice*, refusing to give up on it for sixteen years later. *Pride and Prejudice* finally rose to the literary significance it deserved, despite all of the unfair criticism it received. And Austen rose along with it, finally becoming recognized as one of the greatest authors in history.

F. Scott Fitzgerald

Not only did F. Scott Fitzgerald's *The Great Gatsby* set the literary world on fire by being acclaimed as a great critical success, but the great writer, T.S. Eliot, hailed it as "the first step that American fiction has taken since Henry James." (Eliot, Valerie and Hugh Haughton, eds. *The Letters of T.S. Eliot: Volume 2: 1923-1925.* (New Haven: Yale University Press, 2011), 813.) So great was the influence of *The Great Gatsby*, that, decades after Fitzgerald's passing, the book, released in 1925, was eventually converted into an award-winning movie, featuring Leonardo DiCaprio.

The word of God always seeks trendsetters and life changers. Initially, Fitzgerald's work was not met with great acclaim at all, to the point that publishing icon Charles Scribner said of *The Great Gatsby* that he "could not stomach it at all."

The word, which is of God and thus is God, always wins out beyond any attempt by the shortsightedness of the human ego to stop its release into the world, as the works of Fitzgerald and the world's greatest authors have shown.

In Fitzgerald's case, it took about fourteen hard years of rejection for his own personal word of God to win over the world. But when it did, it won it over big, with his influence carrying on decades beyond his passing. In fact, to this day, *The Great Gatsby* remains one of the most read books at the high school and college level.

Ernest Hemingway

Speaking of Fitzgerald, it wasn't until Fitzgerald contacted legendary editor Maxwell Perkins about Ernest Hemingway, the future winner of the Nobel Prize in Literature, that the soon-to-be icon even got noticed. Perkins had actually rejected the great Fitzgerald in his younger days, as well. This from proves, my perspective, that the divine author in Fitzgerald recognized the brilliance of the divine author in Hemingway. Because, at

"He must forget the things he does not wish to remember and remember only the things he wishes to retain."
BAIRD T. SPALDING
Life and Teaching of the Masters of the Far East

"In the depth of winter, I finally learned that within me there lay an invincible summer."
ALBERT CAMUS

its core, it is the very same author, just writing through the voice of a different human being with different experiences.

And this, of course, brings me to another point. If, as is commonly believed, there are no mistakes and everything does indeed happen for a reason, could your life, like all of the authors mentioned in this section, be providing or have been providing you with the necessary points of reference you need for the backdrop your stories? That was certainly the case with Hemingway, who used his wealth of life experiences and situations as backdrops for the stories he would write. And those stories would go on to change the world.

So, maybe all the years that these authors spent toiling in their crafts were not a waste. Maybe they were just building up understanding of their own individual points of view. Through these, they would then be able to reach their readers, when the divine timing for the release of their books was just right. Could that possibly be true in your life, as well?

J.M. Barrie

J.M. Barrie was an English writer, as well. However, despite the fact that this trendsetter had to pay for the publication of his first book, his worldwide influence may have extended even further than Austen's. Being a trendsetter has its price.

Barrie's foray into the craft began with writing articles. However, that was no more than equivalent to dipping one's toe into a pool. And books cannonball into pools. So, it wasn't unusual that Barrie didn't receive the success his work deserved until he took the leap into books.

Barrie's most acclaimed success, *Peter Pan*, has touched hundreds of millions of lives through not only its

"Fear is that little darkroom where negatives are developed."
MICHAEL PRITCHARD

"The only man who is really free is the one who can turn down an invitation to dinner without giving an excuse."
JULES RENARD

literary representation, but through its movie versions, as well. And not only do those versions continue to live in the hearts of children of all ages, but Barrie's work lives on still, long after his passing, in the psychological condition that bears the name of his most famous character—The Peter Pan Syndrome.

John Steinbeck

Like Barrie, Steinbeck's first real foray into any type of successful writing came from penning articles. And this only came as he tried out the collegiate route to become the author he always felt himself to be, attending Stanford University intermittently for six years, before leaving without a degree in 1925.

By 1927, Steinbeck had taken the step to writing novels. His first few efforts were rejected, not only by the conventional publishing world, but by his overly judgmental personal critic.

Eventually, after his first novel received a wholehearted rejection from many of the top names in the publishing world, the second novel he submitted, *A Life of Sir Henry Morgan*, was finally published. But that did not stop the publishing powers that be from rejecting Steinbeck's next few books for publication.

Finally, in 1935, after ten hard years full of rejection, the world finally caught up with the inspiration represented by Steinbeck's books, as he broke into stardom. He was awarded a Pulitzer Prize for Fiction in 1939 for *The Grapes of Wrath*.

Steinbeck was awarded the Nobel Prize in Literature in 1962, nearly three decades after his efforts began to influence the way we lived and saw the world of the downtrodden. It took nearly thirty years for this world-changing author, most responsible for bringing the

"It is only because I have touched the heart of both joy and pain that I can walk through the doors of compassion."
PAUL FERRINI;
Reflections of the Christ Mind

"Let us be thankful for the fools but for them the rest of us could not succeed."
MARK TWAIN

heartfelt plight of the forgotten into the public view, whose books became the inspiration necessary for so many in the labor movement.

Even today, decades after his passing, his books are still read by the millions each year.

James Joyce

It's amazing how influential and yet, at the same time, completely blind the conventional book publishing industry can be. Even worse, until recently, their usually wayward and always limited thinking held a monopoly over not only us as readers but, even worse, how we thought and what we believed.

In the case of James Joyce, thought by many to be the author of the greatest book of all time, not only was his first book retracted, but it was subsequently rejected, as well.

Despite Joyce's completely unique, mind-expanding style, and in spite of the initial rejection and retraction of his earliest works, the desire of his work to be shared with the world just wouldn't go away.

In fact, his masterpiece, *Ulysses*, took years to get into print. And finally, when it did get published by a tiny English publishing firm, it was banned. The ban, of course, catapulted both the book and Joyce to fame. This illustrates for us how books, as relentless as they all are, will use whatever alternatives are at their disposal, including retraction, rejection, and, most of all, book bans, to get their words out to the world. God is just relentless in that way.

Enough about these old guys and girls, though. Believe me. For each of the stories I have shared about the unwillingness of the word to give up, as it came through from above, there are hundreds of other stories I could have shared, as well. In this chapter, not only did I want to illustrate the relentlessness of the word to be heard, but I also wanted to share how the fall of conventional publishing, as it coincides with the rise of self-publishing, has made it much easier for the word to get itself out. Today, authors can achieve success much less painfully and much more quickly. I include a few vignettes below from contemporary authors, whose stories illustrate this very fact.

Hugh Howey

You may or may not have heard of Hugh Howey. Howey is one of thousands of brand-new, contemporary authors making seven figures a year writing books outside the dying confines of the conventional book publishing arena.

Authors such as Howey, Barbara Freethy (2.8 million book sales), Bella Andre (1.5 million sales), C.J. Lyons (1.3 million sales), and Colleen Hoover (1 million sales) are leading a stampede of first-time authors, side-stepping the inappropriate, and almost always inaccurate, restraining opinions of conventional publishing, and delivering their works directly into the hands of their adoring audiences. (Again, see my book, *Write to Publish*, or view the free video on my website of my class entitled, "The New Age of Publishing.")

In Howey's particular case, his sci-fi thriller, *Wool*, has sold millions of copies and has an almost cult-like following.

"I'm not frightened of the darkness outside. It's the darkness inside houses I don't like."
SHELAGH DELANEY

"If we had no winter, the spring would not be so pleasant; if we did not sometimes taste of adversity, prosperity would not be so welcome."
ANNE BRADSTREET, 1664

E.L. James

The most famous contemporary author to take advantage of this trend, at least initially, was of course, E.L. James, the pen name for self-described "working mom," Erika Mitchell. And behind the long fringe of a rather gawky schoolgirl, she is also the author of *Fifty Shades of Grey*, which has sold more than 200 million copies worldwide in over 52 countries—more than the sales of the entire Harry Potter series combined.

With the type of sales achieved from the sale of her very first book, which has also been made into a movie, one would usually think that Mitchell had gone through all sorts of formal training to reach this level of acclaim. However, the truth is that she began writing *Fifty Shades of Grey* solely after being inspired to start writing by the work of Stephenie Meyer, author of the vampire romance series *Twilight.*

Angels, which are nothing more and nothing less than deliverers of messages, appear in many different shapes and forms. They sometimes even appear as those individuals who challenge us the most. But oftentimes they are all we need to get started. As the deliverer of a message, an angel, in one way or another, brought you to the reading of this book. Maybe he, she, or an event has done so for a reason and that reason is because it is your divine time to shine. Mitchell heard. And she listened when prodded. Maybe you should do so, as well.

By no means is Mitchell a great writer either, proving that you don't even have to be a great writer to achieve literary greatness. All you have to do is be willing to respond when called.

Because of the change in the parameters surrounding the publication of books, Mitchell, even as the novice she was, didn't have to weather the retractions and rejections of those listed above. The availability of modern media to each and every one of us, made it possible or Mitchell to reach her readers directly, without having to go through a cruel, cold, and usually pretentiously long line of editors looking, for a variety of selfish reasons, to put down the eventual brilliance of another. In fact, Mitchell first posted her titillating tale on a *Twilight* fan fiction website, completely devoid of the editorial ignorance so commonplace in conventional publishing. Her fan fiction sparked a word-of-mouth frenzy.

In one way or another, could Erika Mitchell, mild mannered and lacking in literary training, be an illustration of you-in-waiting, to make your God-led impression on the world through the writing of your book?

Got your attention? What do you do now? Turn to the final chapter.

"I believe that anyone can conquer fear by doing the things he fears to do, provided he keeps doing them until he gets a record of successful experiences behind him."

ELEANOR
ROOSEVELT

Note to the Reader:

As you can see from the previous chapters, since the topic has already been covered in my previous writings, this work is not really about how to employ the method to which I refer, to write your book.

Instead, this book is about something possibly even more important. What is the real reason we are drawn to author books and what happens when we make the decision to follow this route using the method to which I refer?

However, I would be remiss were I not to offer you at least an understanding, a start of sorts. The remainder of this book is devoted to showing you a beginning point, by which to commune directly with God through your writing.

I understand that doing so may feel a bit unnerving for you. However, think of it. Would it not be even more unnerving to consider going through your life and not making this connection, especially when it was right at your fingertips?

Please use the remaining chapters as a means to understand the ins and outs of what will transpire on the most magical of all carpet rides. When you embrace this method and utilize it to release the books calling to you through your writing of them, you too will reap the amazing personal benefits available to you.

Read on.

"Touch and be touched. Feel everything. Open your arms to life. That is why you are here."
PAUL FERRINI;
Reflections of the Christ Mind

"The divine spark of awareness keeps your connection with God alive; it connects you to the divine teacher in your tradition and to the divinity within your brothers and sisters."
PAUL FERRINI;
Reflections of the Christ Mind

Chapter Ten
A Psychology Class That Changed
My Life as an Author

As I mentioned in the first chapter on My Story, when I was first introduced to the method for both the writing and publishing of a book, that I have been sharing now for over three decades, the vision that I received awoke me in the middle of the night, and initially came to me as my life passing before my eyes. It was an answer to my prayers in response to my request on how to succeed at both the writing and publishing of books. And it included selective elements regarding the answer to my prayers. Thus, only certain aspects of my life were included. However, in response to all that I was shown in the vision, I could certainly see that I had been, and *how* I had been, prepared for that moment and time. I was prepared to make my major leap forward. No stone had been left unturned.

However, what surprised me the most was that the concentration of the vision I was receiving centered, not around what I had learned directly about writing up to that point, but instead on what I had learned through my courses in psychology, all of which I had been magically drawn to. For once my desire to take class after class in psychology actually made sense. From that vision, I could actually see how my psychology classes had taught me what I really needed to know about writing. Whereas, my writing courses had led me astray—and I mean way astray. In fact, looking back after having discovered the truth about the art form, I would have to say that over 95 percent of what I had learned, read, or been taught about writing was completely the opposite of what I discovered to be true. So, from my learned perspective, if you would

"If he should but realize that every idea is a direct expression from God and, as soon as this idea comes to him, he would immediately make it his ideal to be expressed from God, then take his mortal hands off, and let God express through him the perfect way, this ideal would come through perfect."

BAIRD T. SPALDING;
Life and Teaching of the Masters of the Far East

just consistently do the exact opposite of what you had read, learned, or been taught about writing, you would pretty much be on the right track to getting to where you aspired to be as an author.

At the epicenter of our deepest misunderstanding about the actual essence of writing is the belief that one had to be visited by a so-called Muse to experience expressive, oftentimes artistic, enlightenment. Of course, it was thought that this Muse, who lived outside of us, visited if and when, and only if and when, it wanted to do so.

And there was no way that one could call the Muse. No way. For the Muse supposedly based its decision on whether or not to visit itself upon the writer on some sort of unachievable worthiness. Of course, if that certain potentially superstitious form of worthiness was actually needed before the so-called Muse would visit a simple human being, surely David the Adulterer, Moses the Murderer, and the mere carpenter's son, Christ, would have never been chosen for a visit. So, that kind of disputes that contention.

Plus, despite all of the tremendous theories and facets of understanding they offered to life, it is important to keep in mind that the actual concept of the so-called Muse was created by the Ancient Greeks. And despite, all of the greatness they offered to life, this is the civilization that also openly and strongly encouraged the practice of older men sleeping with younger boys, which, of course, is now classified as sexual molestation. (Dawson, *Cities of the Gods*, p. 193. See also George Boys-Stones, "Eros in Government: Zeno and the Virtuous City," *Classical Quarterly* 48 (1998), 168–174) So, despite the guiding light that they provided in so many other aspects of culture, the Ancient Greeks could be wrong on occasion. They were certainly incorrect in their concept of a so-called "outside Muse" having to visit an individual in order for one to gain enlightenment. Dead wrong, in fact.

For it was a belief in this accepted concept, which led many a worth-seeking artist, author, or actor to the dysfunctional life style of drink, drug, or overt sexuality. These individuals often found their early grave, waiting for the so-called Muse to show up.

It was Roger Sperry who finally put any substance on this Muse theory to rest with his work which began in the late sixties.

Sperry had a distinct compassion for epileptics, who suffered from often life-threatening, grand mal seizures. He decided to surgically sever the *corpus callosum* in certain willing epileptic patients to see if doing so would halt the severity of their seizures. The *corpus callosum* is an interconnected network of nerves that allowed, as was believed at the time, the right and left lobes of a person's brain to communicate. The basic principle behind taking this step was that, by severing their *corpus callosum*, a grand mal seizure would be stopped from spreading between the left and right lobes. This surely transpired in Sperry's work with his patients.

However, Sperry stumbled upon a discovery that was far greater than anything he'd had in mind at the time. Not only did Sperry discover through his work that human beings, in fact, had two individual brains, as opposed to two lobes of the same brain, as previously believed. He also discovered that the seat and access point of the so-called Muse actually lay right inside each one of us. And in the vast majority of us, it is located in the right brain. So, in essence, Sperry discovered that all one had to do to gain what he thought was artistic enlightenment was to access one's right brain. Doing so would lead to a direct, inspirational connection to the Divine.

Now, there are several ways to achieve this transference of consciousness, including life and body-destroying modalities, such as alcohol and drugs, as well as involuntary events, such as near-death experiences and

"Pain is inevitable. Suffering is optional."
M. KATHLEEN CASEY

"Hope is the feeling you have that the feeling you have isn't permanent."
JEAN KERR

life-threatening diseases. Many of these are described in detail in any number of wonderful, life changing books, such as Betty Edwards' *Drawing on the Right Side of the Brain* (Tarcher, 1978) or Gabrielle Rico's *Writing the Natural Way* (Tarcher, 1983).

But in essence, with his Split-Brain Theory, for which he won a Nobel Prize in Physiology and Medicine in 1981, Sperry showed us how we could voluntarily achieve enlightenment through writing. We do so by accessing the so-called Muse; and in most of us this is located in our right brain. All of this I learned in a routine college psychology class—the best writing class I ever took.

How does all of this work?

Easy. You simply fool a part of your brain, or put half of it to sleep through a relaxation exercise. Which half? In most of us, this is the left brain, which is mostly comprised of our intellectual and dominant brain. When that transpires, the right brain, which is directly connected to the Divine, comes streaming through into our consciousness.

Chapter Eleven

A Quick Summation of How the Most Divine of All Connections is Established Through Writing

As I mentioned earlier, I am not going to go into any sort of lengthy dissertation in regard to writing a book, or how to do so in a weekend. That is already covered in some of my previous works. However, I do feel that it is only fair that I at least cover the basics on how this most divine of all connections can once again be established in your life.

To do so, you don't need to work long and hard. You don't need to struggle or fight. You don't need to live in an ashram in India and study meditation for years upon years. No. And it doesn't matter one bit what leads you to the point of deciding to take this step. For me, like so many who want more out of their lives and eventually attend one of my retreats, it was desperation, which finally led me to open up to the greater greatness of God. It may have been faith that has led you to this step, or a combination of both desperation and faith. As I mentioned, it doesn't matter what got you here. All that matters is that you have arrived.

Again, you don't need to devote a lot of time to take this step effectively, because you will be creating a brand new state for yourself. No. Instead, you will simply be returning to an innate state that already exists; one that you will instantly recognize on a soul level. You can proactively achieve this state rather easily and quickly, as I will show.

*"Every good thought
you think is contributing
its share to the ultimate
result of your life."*
GRENVILLE KLEISER

What I share below is the exact procedure that I have been offering aspiring authors for decades as a solution to writer's block. Writer's block, of course, is nothing more than a cerebral reaction, or better—a resistance—to achievement of this ultimate of all states through writing. The reason your left brain or mind resists this process is because of ego, which falsely identifies itself as your God. And, of course, if you make that ultimate of all connections, your ego will be displaced in your life as the God it wants to be for you. Your ego resists the process.

Thank God, no pun intended, for our sake that the left brain, or mind, sleeps, while the right brain, or heart, never does. Since the basic root of the latter is Divine, like God, it does not need to sleep. While the left, being more human in nature, does become exhausted and needs to sleep. The difference between the two sides is at the very essence of our abilities to proactively achieve this most divine of all states.

To easily achieve this state, all one has to do is ease the mind toward sleep, which is quite easy to do. When the left brain or mind, which our culture has made dominant in our lives, falls to sleep, the more powerful, but subordinated, heart or right brain can take control of our consciousness. Then, and only then, will we experience direct oneness with our Creator and our most natural selves that we all seek.

How do you do this?

Simple. And like I mentioned, you can self-induce this connected state in only minutes, any time you choose.

First, pick a time when you know you will be undisturbed for at least thirty minutes. Or if you are writing a book (see my book, *You Can Write a Book in a Weekend*), you may want to reserve hours or days of time.

Setting time aside when you will be undisturbed is not only the step to take, but also the most essential of all steps. Because you don't want anyone interrupting your conversation with God, especially not while you are listening to Him/Her/It.

Second, after you have set aside your time to commune with the Source, from Whom you are a direct descendant, go to my website at tombird.com. On the home page of my site you will see a Freebie icon. Click on it and scroll down the page until you get to the free download of the *Transitioning Back to the Author You Were Meant to Be* CD. Download it for free and take time to review the different tracks.

Third, begin the time you have set aside to commune with God, play the six-minute relaxation track of the CD and follow the instructions.

Fourth, after you have listened to the track featuring the relaxation techniques, which is designed to put your left brain to sleep, switch to the subliminal track.

The subliminal track is designed to keep you in the God-connected state by stimulating your right brain. Meanwhile, the music is devoid of rhythm and serves to keep the left brain asleep. You can play this hour-long track over and over and over again, for as many times as you would like to stay in this state, for however long you choose.

Personally, I turn on the subliminal track of the CD as soon as I enter my office each working day and I don't turn it off until I leave. Doing so puts me in the essential state of listening, which is nothing more and nothing less than meditation. It is nothing more than a state of listening, and easily accessible through this free CD, which can lead you back to connect with the Source from which you sprang, God.

"The world is charged with the grandeur of God."
GERARD MANLEY HOPKINS

"He who has a why to live can hear almost any how."
NIETZSCHE

Chapter Twelve
How Others Have Connected

Because God is always reaching out to us, and because we are one with Him/Her/It as a result of being the direct offspring of this Source, the ways in which we can form a direct communion are limitless. For God always seeks to connect with us and is willing to meet with us wherever we are willing to meet with God. Just like the radios in our cars, we can tune in on a vast selection of channels. The only difference being that, with God, the number of stations is unlimited.

However, the essential component that must be present for us to be able to accept a direct connection with God into our lives is that our left brains must be quieted. For the majority of us, the left brain is our controlling cerebral side. By quieting the left brain, the right brain, which, for the majority of us, comprises a direct connection to Source, can then inhabit our consciousness. God can then be heard, whether that means actually heard, felt, seen, or by any other means we have to experience God.

Because the conscious quieting of the left brain was not an accepted component of entering into a so-called inspirational, creative, or muse state (terms formally used to describe the result of this divine union) until the time of Roger Sperry, people sought to reach this state or entered into it through a myriad of voluntary and involuntary methods.

In the late sixties and early seventies, legendary cult icon Timothy Leary achieved this higher connection through the use of mind-altering LSD. And he was far from the first to do so. Artists, actors, and authors of all

"Here is the test to find whether your mission on earth is finished: If you're alive, it isn't."
RICHARD BACH

"We never do anything 'til we cease to think about the manner of doing it."
WILLIAM HAZLITT

kinds, including Edgar Allan Poe, Jack Kerouac, and Ernest Hemingway, just to name a few, have used all kinds of substances in an attempt to propel them out of their left brains and into this consciousness spurred by the desperate need to create, but later by addiction to these substances they used to jolt themselves into divine connection.

Madness is also a way to make this transition of pushing away the left brain to make room for the right. Of course, the price that one pays to make the shift in this manner is extreme.

Our physical response to music is another means to enter into this most divine of all states. Letting oneself go through the exertion of dance wears out the physical body to the point where the left brain responds by drifting off to sleep. The right brain and its divine connection can then take over.

In fact, all extreme flowing physical exercise works in this manner. This explains why great athletes, such as Michael Jordan, often end up taking over a game, or playing their best games after the onset of physical fatigue, or in response to becoming physically ill. In this state of fatigue or illness, they are unable to maintain a rigorous mental state.

There are several other ways to achieve this state involuntarily, including meditation and taking a long drive in the car. These activities allow the right brain to access one's consciousness by putting the left brain to sleep. You can also go to sleep and wake up, either mid-sleep or in the middle of the night, in a right brain state, while the left brain still slumbers.

In reality, there are an unlimited number of tactics through which we can return to and achieve this innate state. And by no means am I saying that writing is the only way to achieve this state—far from it. What I am saying is that we can self-induce this state at will by creating the necessary ingredients by which to write from this state. A real reason so many of us are drawn to write, especially books, may be because that's God's way of getting us to connect directly with Him/Her/It. Our draw to write may be God's way of getting us to return to our own divine roots.

Chapter Thirteen
Once There

Once in the ultimate of all listening states, you have God's ear. And God's ear is always open to you. But even more importantly, He/She/It has your ear. Let the conversation begin!

Even though many of us assume that God can hear us, we forget that we can hear God, as well. Thus, upon entering this state, the ultimate of all conversations can begin. And every good conversation begins with a question.

With your eyes closed and your chin dropped to your chest, as is suggested in the relaxation track of the CD you have hopefully downloaded by now, just for practice, ask the following questions one at a time.

After you have asked these questions, and responded to them in longhand, preferably on large, lineless sheets of paper, start to make up questions of your own. Ask anything you'd like. Just remember to remain calm and quiet after asking a question, not only so that you can potentially hear the response, but more importantly so that you can feel the response come to you.

After doing so, open up your eyes, lift your chin from your chest, pick up your pen, and start writing. Keep in mind while writing to: a) Write as fast as you can—doing so will not only ostracize your obsessive mind from taking over, but keep your connection with God flowing as a result. b) Refrain from reading what you are writing. If you choose to do so, it will throw you into a judgmental state of being. c) Always write what you feel, no matter what it is. This will keep you connected to God through the only place open enough for Him/Her/It to come fully through—your heart. And d) keep your pen moving at all times, even if that translates to scribbling. For if the pen stops, so does the inspiration pouring through you, and so does your connection with God.

Here are the sample questions I suggest you start off asking, one at a time, while in this most blessed of all states:

Why is it that I am drawn to writing?
What is it that I am meant to write?
What is it that I am meant to write now?

Chapter Fourteen
Common Responses to the Aforementioned Exercise

Even with the innateness of our connection to God, and as badly as we both want to re-establish this relationship on a permanent basis, just like any relationship, some start off slow and gain momentum and some just start out fast. Expect nothing more and nothing less in re-establishing this relationship. Be patient with yourself if the communication begins slowly or even feels totally blocked. This is surely not reflective of God's desire or ability to connect with you. Beginning slowly is simply reflective of how open or closed you are to God, and thus how much He/She/It has to move out of the way to be able to fully reach you.

When Eckhart Tolle consciously began his spiritual quest, he sat silently on the same park bench, each day at the same time, often for hours. In doing so, Tolle, in sort of a *Waiting for Godot* approach, was making unadulterated time for God to communicate to him. And so, Tolle waited and waited and waited, and the rest is history. Tolle's life totally changed when he began hearing God and then allowing God to move into him, and then out into the world through his life. He went from being an average human being, living an average life, to a world-changing, bestselling author.

In essence, I am suggesting you do something similar, but in a vastly more efficient and effective manner. Start out, like Tolle, by picking a time. Initially hours are not necessary. But thirty minutes would be nice. Then, first, actively remove any left brain barriers between you and

"If you have anything really valuable to contribute to the world it will come through the expression of your own personality, that single spark of divinity that gets you off and makes you different from every other living creature."
BRUCE BARTON

"It is only the farmer who faithfully plants seeds in the Spring, that reaps a harvest in the Autumn."
B. C. FORBES

God, by relaxing or, even better, following the suggestions for doing so on the relaxation portion of my free CD. You will then be in an active receiving mode. Secondly, while in an active receiving mode, you will be reaching up to meet God through the vibration level associated with writing fast. And third, you will be maintaining that connection by continuing to write fast.

If you would like to substantially accelerate the process and clear out any personal resistance that could keep you from moving more smoothly, more quickly with this process, and, thus, receiving more fluid results more quickly, I suggest reading and doing the exercises in my book, *Write to Heal*—the smallest, but most powerful, book I have ever written. *Write to Heal* is mandatory pre-reading for anyone taking one of my retreats. Your results from working through the book will surface instantly. With their personal barriers to the Source removed, the books seeking to be written by aspiring authors at my retreats pour right out of them from the get go. The same goes for those I personally lead through this exercise. In their cases, I literally lift them over their usually self-imposed barriers. On your own, the results you may experience may not be as fluid, which is why, if you would like things to flow more smoothly—especially from the beginning—I suggest you may want to strongly consider reading and doing the exercises in *Write to Heal*.

So, in regard to your personal responses to the exercises presented in the last chapter, you may have:

Responded fluidly and tuned into the answers for all three questions;
Responded fluidly to some, but not all, of them; or
Responded fluidly to none of them.

> *"Thinking has become a disease. Disease happens when things get out of balance."*
> ECKHART TOLLE
> *The Power of Now*

> *"Where were you fellows when the paper was blank?"*
> FRED ALLEN

> *"He is not busy being born; he is busy dying."*
> BOB DYLAN

If you responded fluidly to all three questions, do nothing. Based upon your results, you are probably already attuned and clear.

However, if your writing was slow, choppy, or stagnant with any of the three questions, I suggest that you do two things:

Revisit the step-by-step approach to this exercise that was laid out in Chapter Thirteen. See if you followed the instructions to a tee. If not, therein probably lies the reason for the choppiness of follow-through. If that's the case, simply follow the instructions more closely, moving forward. And as you do, you will see marked improvement.

If you did follow the instructions to a tee and your response was still choppy or non-existent, it's probably because you still have a lot of personal baggage clogging up the hallway between you and God. If that's the case, you don't have to invest in any time-consuming and expensive psychotherapy or anything like that. Just pick up a copy of *Write to Heal*, read it, and do the exercises. Doing so will reopen for you the most essential of all passageways.

"The door is never closed to you or anyone else."
PAUL FERRINI;
Reflections of the Christ Mind

"America's best buy is a telephone call to the right man."
ILKA CHASE

Chapter Fifteen
Practice Makes Perfect

Before moving on, I suggest that you:

Work on perfecting your communion connection with God, using the suggestions made at the end of Chapter Fourteen;

Take some time, a week or longer, if you would prefer, to follow the routine described previously to perfect your technique;

And, while doing so, come up with a list of questions to ask of God on your own.

As covered earlier, for further instruction on how to write or publish a book, I suggest that you visit my other books, such as *You Can Write Your Book in a Weekend* and *Write to Publish*.

"We do not write in order to be understood; we write to understand."
C. DAY LEWIS
The Poetic Image

"He is his own best friend and takes delight in privacy; whereas the man of no virtue or ability is his own worst enemy and is afraid of solitude."
ARISTOTLE

Chapter Sixteen
What do you do now?

Thank you for taking this long journey through this short book with me.

During our journey together, hopefully you have gained a much better understanding as to what your potential draw to writing a book truly represents. As well, I hope you have obtained a better sense of how to merge with the transformational magic associated with the ultimate of all states of communion, represented by the method which I have been led to share.

However, for you, the question remains: What do you do now?

In response, first of all, let me state that what you do or choose not to do is totally up to you. There is no right or wrong, only what you feel is right or wrong for you at this time.

You can choose to write a book or not write one. You can choose to write one with me at one of my retreats or go it alone or with a group of friends. It's totally up to you what you do.

But a bit of last-minute advice for you.

If those around you are encouraging you to write a book; if your mind is constantly wandering off in the direction of best seller lists; if you are a voluntary, avid reader of books; if an inspiration to write overtakes you, for whatever reason, at a variety of times and places, these are all signs that you have a divinely-led and conceived book or books inside of you, that are trying to be born through you.

"I am in the present. I cannot know what tomorrow will bring forth. I can know only what the truth is for me today. That is what I am called upon to serve, and I serve it in all lucidity."
IGOR STRAVINSKY, 1936

"It is only when we take things into our own hands that the problems and difficulties begin. This is not for one, or a few, this is for all."
BAIRD T. SPALDING; *Life and Teaching of the Masters of the Far East*

From my experience, these are all books that were co-authored by you and God on the other side of life and all were meant to be born during this, your present, lifetime.

You can either choose to birth your book(s) or not. You have the free will to make that decision on your own.

Just remember though, that should you decide not to go the route of the divine author, the desire of your book(s) will not dissipate. And they will continue to nag you for the rest of your days. Sorry to be such a bearer of bad news. It has simply been my experience that once a commitment is made on the other side, it remains committed no matter what resistance it runs into.

Should you, though, decide to birth your book(s), your life will burst open like a balloon, and you will be taken to places as a divine human being that you never could have imagined you would ever go. As you commune directly with the Source from which we were all spawned, you will contribute to this thing called life in amazingly influential ways. Personally, you will love more deeply, express more authentically, and feel and experience more abundantly than you ever thought possible.

Another last-minute bit of advice—if you desire to take the step to become an author using the method which I share, treat your desire to write with the great respect it deserves. Don't limit your journey by going cheap on it with your commitment. This is one glorious area in which you get out of the situation ten-fold what you put into it. Authoring is a big-play league. Either go big or go home. Again, it's your choice how you play it.

With all of that in mind, if you decide to take this step, don't let this day pass without taking a major step toward making this driven goal a tangible reality in your life. For your book, your divine author, your divine destiny, and, most of all, God are all waiting.

"In the beginning was the Word, and the Word was with God, and the Word was God." - John 1:1.

Made in the USA
Middletown, DE
05 February 2016